The A.D.D. and A.D.H.D. DIET!

A comprehensive look at contributing factors
and natural treatments
for symptoms of

Attention Deficit Disorder
and
Hyperactivity

by
Rachel Bell and Dr. Howard Peiper

Foreword by Doris Rapp, M.D.

Published by SAFE GOODS
East Canaan, CT

The A.D.D. and A.D.H.D. DIET!
by
Rachel Bell and Dr. Howard Peiper

Copyright© 1997 by Rachel Bell and Dr. Howard Peiper

ISBN 1-884820-29-8-50995
Library of Congress Catalog Card Number 97-66518
Printed in the United States of America
1st Printing June, 1997
7th Printing June 2000
Revised Edition

Edited by Nina Anderson

The A.D.D. and A.D.H.D. DIET is not intended as medical advice. It is written solely for informational and educational purposes. Please consult a health professional should the need for one be indicated.

Published by SAFE GOODS
283 East Canaan Rd.
East Canaan, CT 06024
(860)-824-5301

Preface

Attention Deficit Disorder (ADD) and Attention Deficit Hyperactivity Disorder (ADHD) are diagnosed more often now than ever before. Increased awareness about these conditions may contribute, in part, to the rise in documented cases. Other reasons may include, changes in our diets, lack of essential nutrients, greater exposure to both indoor and outdoor air pollution, and increased exposure to biologically active agents in our food and water supplies. Unfortunately, solutions aren't happening fast enough, as witnessed by the gross numbers of people still suffering, of which several million of these are children.

The symptoms of ADD/ADHD are manifestations of a dysfunction of the central nervous system. The patterns of imbalance observed in these disorders vary from person to person in an individualized, *person-specific,* constellation of symptoms, as follows.

Behavioral
short attention span
inability to focus or concentrate
inability to sit still
uncontrollable limbs
shifting from one uncompleted activity to another
tendency to be easily distracted
difficulty following instructions
difficulty sustaining attention to tasks
difficulty playing quietly
appearing not to listen
forgetfulness
irritability and anxiousness
compulsive, aggressive, destructive behavior
head knocking
temper tantrums
passivity
withdrawn demeanor
difficulty communicating feelings

Cognitive
slow learning and reasoning ability
lessened perceptual and conceptual ability
impairment of language and memory skills
dyslexia

Social
difficulty getting along with other people
avoided by other people
tendency to interrupt
tendency to talk too much, too loud, too fast
tendency to blurt out whatever comes to mind
difficulty awaiting turn

Muscular
poor motor control
tendency to be accident prone

People with ADD/ADHD may be fine one minute and "off the wall" the next. This apparent random type of behavior may not be random at all. It may be caused by food or environmental allergens. It could be due to a blood sugar disturbance, mineral imbalance, or the presence of toxic metals at the cellular level. It could be caused by any of a number of things. But it most certainly is not mere coincidence.

A Note From the Authors

Writing about this subject is challenging. On the one hand there is the need to be calm, cool, and collected. To present the material in a professional manner. On the other hand, the children are growing up and there is no time to waste being overly polite. What thought, if any, is going into making the world a better place for them? What degree of dedication do we have toward their health and well being? We are living by habit, most of us. To live life differently is inconceivable to some. To think that we have a choice in the matter, to think that if we want to, we can change the course of our lives and do it differently, is new to many. How do we change even if we know we can? How do we do it? How do we change all that we are? Or some of what we are? Or enough of what we are to lessen the pain that we may feel inside? How do we find peace of mind?

The things we discuss in this book, affect us all. We are inextricably tied together. There is a state of emergency concerning the lives of our children. ADD/ADHD is not just something that "happens" to some people. It is not something that you have to "learn to live with," or something that, "you can't do anything about." You **can** do something about it. We have written this book to show you how.

Foreword

It is presently estimated that from 8 to 22 million children may be placed on activity-modifying drugs, such as Ritalin by the year 2000. Of this group, 20 to 40% will not be helped. Many believe what educators and physicians have told them. Namely, that there are no choices other than drugs and psychotherapy.

Drugs should be the last choice in treating an illness, especially when the drugs come with a long list of side effects. Alternative forms of therapy should certainly be considered before any child is placed on a drug that is similar to cocaine. The first choice should be to detect and eliminate the cause of the illness. Common causes for symptoms of ADD and ADHD are favorite foods and/or contact with dust, mold, pollen and chemicals. These types of exposures bring about complaints such as fatigue, headaches, intestinal problems, muscle aches, recurrent infections, bed wetting, hayfever, asthma, hives and learning and behavioral problems. The proper use of nutrients often enables the body to withstand adverse environmental exposures and problematic foods with much less difficulty.

As this book details, nutrients are unquestionably helpful for many and eliminating highly allergenic foods, can sometimes totally relieve hyperactivity or ADD in 3-7 days. A growing number of Americans are finding out what English, European, South American and Indian physicians have known for a long time. Homeopathy, herbs, flower remedies, and techniques such as acupuncture all may reduce symptoms.. An adjustment by a well trained osteopathic or chiropractic practitioner may correct misalignment of the structure of the body which has lead to forms of illness that cannot be corrected with a quieting drug. These options are usually both safe and effective and many times relieve some symptoms on a permanent basis.

ADD and ADHD reflect much more than a physical and emotional illness. We also must realize that our basic values and priorities in life often directly influence how we feel and act. When both patients and physicians recognize and address this aspect of illness, we should all enjoy more optimum health.

—Doris Rapp., M.D.

Clinical Assistant Professor of Pediatrics at SUNYAB and Author of *"Is This Your Child's World?"* and the video *"Environmentally Sick Schools"*

"They could have done it, the Carthaginians. Or the Etruscans, or the Egyptians. Four thousand years ago, five thousand years ago, they could have flown . . . It was possible, all those years ago, it could have been done. But it wasn't. Nobody applied the principles of flight because nobody understood them and nobody understood them because nobody believed flight was possible for human beings."—Richard Bach from A Gift of Wings

Thank you Nina and Charly, Karen, Michael, Chrissy, and little Anna, and not so little Emily.

Special thanks to

Dr. Marshall Mandell, Dr. Doris Rapp, Laurene Procacinni, R.N., Dr. Billie Jay Sahley, Ph.D., and Dr. Esteban Genao

Table of Contents

Chapter 1

If You Want Something Different You've Got to Do Something Different

If you are reading this book, chances are you either have ADD or ADHD or you know someone who does. You may be curious about alternative, non-drug (and free from drug side effects) methods of treating ADD/ADHD. This book has been written to give you the latest information. We want you to understand what the best informed professionals know—ADD and ADHD can be effectively treated through natural means that address the causes and contributing factors of these reversible conditions. Diet definitely plays a part. You may have had some enlightening experiences with this already. Or you may not. Either way, you're not alone.

If you, or a person that you care about, have ADD or ADHD what could you be looking for? More energy? Less energy? A greater ability to focus? Increased attention span? To comprehend what you are reading? To improve your job performance? To attain better health? What would you be willing to do to get what you want?

Would you . . .
Eat more vegetables?
Eat more protein and less sugar?
Take vitamins, minerals, or amino acids?
Avoid the foods that cause problems for you?
Seek out the care of knowledgeable professionals who could help you get what you want?

Where Are You Now?

Do you have a little problem or a big problem? Do you need a lot of help right away or a little help over a longer period of time?

For some people, ADD or ADHD has taken over their life (and perhaps their family's life, too) and has become an unbearable nightmare affecting virtually every imaginable situation. For others the problem is confined to an inability to focus on schoolwork or to sit still for long periods of time. Knowing how much help you need will help you determine how dedicated you want to become at finding solutions.

Where do You Want to Be?

Do you have an idea of how you would like your life to be? How about the life of the affected person you care about? Is it different from the way your life (their life) is now?

Creating a clear picture in your mind of what you want is a very important step toward getting it. Sometimes we don't know exactly what we want, but we do know we want things to get better.

Knowing that you want things to be better is important, but it will be more helpful if you can be specific. For example, you could say, "I want two things to change: I want to learn to control my unpredictable temper and I want to eat foods that make me feel healthy." This is being specific, and it will help you get what you want.

If you are a parent making these decisions for your child, then you have two choices. You may either involve your child in the goal setting by asking them what they would like to work on first, or you may choose goals for them if the child is very young.

For example, you may decide that you want to work together with your child to accomplish the following goals:

2

1. Learn which foods or environmental factors are causing a problem.
2. Replace those factors with safe alternatives.
3. Help the child gain an ability to focus.

These are just examples. Right now would be a good time for you to think of a few things that you would like to accomplish in your life related to your ADD (or your child's ADD or ADHD) and write them down. Just grab the nearest scrap of paper and jot down a few sentences. They don't even have to be sentences, they could just be words. Writing things down is important. It helps us get what we want. If you can't find a scrap of paper, use the space below.

1.

2.

3.

There, now you have some goals. This is a good start, because now you have something specific to work towards. This is a great first step. The second step is to decide not to quit. After that, it's a journey to success.

Do not quit and you will find the answers you need. We wrote this book to help you. Sometimes learning something new can seem overwhelming in the beginning because there is so much to learn. We will take things one easy step at a time and this way it will not be overwhelming.

How to use this Book
Each chapter will tell you what you need to know about the subject(s) of that chapter. Then you will be able to decide what you should do based on the information we give you. You have made an important decision to read this book. It can help you achieve the goals you have set.

Chapter 2

Going Through the Open Door

"It is one thing to be able to see an open door, but it is quite another to be able to walk through it."—Olivia Franklin

One of the most common problems that people face in changing the way they eat and live is that it may require a great deal of effort. It is especially difficult within a family structure where all members of the family may not feel excited about participating.

We get used to living a certain way and it is hard to change. Even so, it is important for family members to support one another. Research shows that attempts to modify the diet and lifestyle of children with ADD or ADHD are rarely successful unless the parents are willing to change, also.

Change is sometimes difficult, but in these serious circumstances the results will be well worth the effort. The future course of a life—and the lives of many others—is at stake.

"If Johnny would just try harder"

Parents, teachers and bosses often make the mistake of assuming that the person with ADD or ADHD needs to **try harder**. This situation can lead to increased frustration for everyone involved. Those with ADD/ADHD *are* trying hard, but *trying* is not the same as *being able to do*. In some instances, *doing* is actually temporarily impossible. As difficult as this may be to believe at times, it is true.

The following story illustrates this point. This is a true story based on an experiment that was done with a dog in a cage. It concerned the dog's learned response to electrical shock, but it speaks to us all concerning what has become normal in our lives, and about how we act once that has happened. Dr. Deepak Chopra tells it very well, and we heard it from him. The message it brings should help your understanding of what it's like to be unable to save yourself even though the answer to the problem may be obvious to everyone else.

The experiment went like this. A dog was placed in a cage. One corner of the cage was rigged to deliver an electric shock when stepped on and so the dog learned very quickly to avoid that area.

Eventually the entire floor of the cage was electrified. This made the dog completely helpless, unable to find a safe place anywhere. The dog cried for a while and then simply gave up. It stopped trying to communicate. But that is not the most interesting part.

The most interesting part is that when the door of the cage was opened, the dog would not leave. Even though it was free to go, it had learned that it was unable to help itself. It had learned to surrender to the pain, to give up the struggle, and to abandon hope. Its abnormal situation had become normal. The dog had forgotten why it wanted to get out of the cage.

This is what it is like to have ADD/ADHD. You know what people want you to do because you can hear them telling you what it is, but you can't *do* it. Sometimes the confusion in the brain is so awful that the person with ADD/ADHD doesn't even know what you mean, really, when you say, "Sit in that chair." As with Alzheimer's. What chair? What is a chair?

On the one hand, people with ADD or ADHD want very much to do what will please their teacher or their parents or their boss, but on the other hand they *don't know how*. Even though the open door is staring them boldly in the face, it is nearly impossible to get up and walk through it. They can't remember how to do that kind of walking. Something else has become normal and to get through that door seems impossible.

This is often where the frustration becomes unbearable for parents and others who want to help. People often make the mistake of thinking that good advice and loving kindness, praise, encouragement, soothing words, or pointing in a certain direction, are all that are needed to get someone to change or to behave. Although this definitely helps, sometimes it just isn't enough. When a person becomes "difficult to reach," or seems "tuned out," the problem may be a biochemical one.

Dr. Marshall Mandell, founder of the New England Center for Allergic & Environmental Diseases, understands this. He points out that although tips given to teachers, parents, and even bosses "appear reasonable" they are really "Of little importance when an ADD or ADHD brain has become an allergic battlefield and it cannot function in a manner that permits the [person] to understand and absorb what's going on. Threats of restrictions or punishment are also useless, because a malfunctioning brain can't remember the consequences of prohibited behavior."

This explains what happens when a child with ADHD is given an instruction such as, "All you have to do is sit still and be quiet." The instruction is like that open door, go through it and everything will be different, life will get better. But such an instruction is meaningless. What is "sit still and be quiet." What is, "go through the door." No, you must sit me still and be me quiet. You must put me through the door. Let me experience it so I know what to shoot for next time.

Therefore, the conditions of nutrition, diet, and environment have to change, *and* the learned behavior may *also* have to change. Sometimes the avoidance or removal of triggering factors automatically precipitates a change of behavior, but not always.

Children, (or grown ups for that matter), may at first be violently opposed to making changes in their diet. However, studies show that once the person has experienced a positive result, there is more ability, as well as willingness, to cooperate. The objective is to relieve the symptoms by removing the cause. This will *give the person with ADD/ADHD an experience of clarity of thought*. This may be all that is required to provide the person with the knowledge of what to aim for in the future. Sort of like opening a window of opportunity so they can see where they're going.

The equivalent action in the case of the dog in the electric cage would be to remove the dog from its cage. The dog will know that something is different. Eventually, with the proper care, it will learn to want *not* to be electrocuted any longer. The dog will be able to regain its ability to avoid pain just as the person with ADD/ADHD will be able to gain or regain the ability to decipher between what is clear thinking/behavior and what is not. In many cases, people will continue to choose the clear thinking/ behavior once they have taken the opportunity to experience it. If it is a child's behavior that you wish to change and the child continues to be uncooperative, even after he or she has experienced clear thinking/behavior, then perhaps more changes in the family diet and lifestyle may be required.

In reading this book, you will learn about ways to treat ADD or ADHD naturally. You will learn about the contributing and causal factors. You may find, as you read, that you are developing a clearer understanding of the complexity of life, and a deeper appreciation for all living things.

Chapter 3

"But Why Do I Have ADD?"

Many people with ADD or ADHD are very intelligent, always thinking of new possibilities and ways to make things better. Albert Einstein, Thomas Edison, and Winston Churchill are classic examples, and there are dozens of others. In special schools for children with ADD/ADHD this point is stressed as a method of increasing self esteem as the child struggles to cope with the problem. However, this is only a partial answer, at best. What must eventually be addressed are the underlying causes of ADD/ADHD. These causes are *biological* in origin.

The inability to get along in school is not necessarily the sign of a failure for life. Some people simply march to the beat of a different drum. Thomas Edison, for example, was said to be uneducable. He attended less than six months of formal schooling, but by doing things his own way, Edison became a great inventor. Unfortunately this is not the case with everyone who has ADD/ADHD. In many instances, the person with ADD/ADHD is unable to *use* his or her unique gifts or talents because the symptoms of ADD or ADHD get in the way.

Anyone *can* succeed, but there is no way to predict *who* that will be. Our prisons are full of people whose attempts at doing things differently were not so well received. Most prisoners say they had trouble getting along in school. It has been suggested that many of them may have suffered from undiagnosed cases of ADD or ADHD as children. The diagnosis may never have been made because of a lack of knowledge about the condition. ADD, ADHD, LD, school failure, drop out, newer and bigger prisons, escalating violence and crime rate amongst children—what is the connection to health? Why do so many more people have ADD/ADHD now than ever before? Why are many people sick, tired, moody, irritable, and depressed?

To a great degree, the contributing and/or causative factors lie in our lifestyles—our dietary and environmental exposures. Most of us know we could be eating better. We know that air and water quality cannot be taken for granted any longer. We know that these factors are affecting our health. And we know that we can change our ways if we want to. It is up to the grownups to make the necessary changes that will ensure clean air, nutritious food, and pure water for all the generations to follow. The children would do it if they could, but they can't—not without our complete and immediate cooperation.

The following factors present a number of causes of ADD/ADHD and begin to point us in a positive direction concerning treatment.

1. **Poor Nutrition**
    a. intake of fresh foods is down
    b. soil is depleted of essential nutrients, therefore, fresh foods that we do eat, may have less nutritional value than we may think
    c. intake of highly processed foods containing additives, preservatives, and artificial chemical colorings and flavorings is up - way up
    d. vitamin, mineral, enzyme, amino acid, neurotransmitter, and essential fatty acid deficiencies growing worse with each generation

2. **Environmental contaminants**
    a. insecticide and pesticide residues in our food and water
    b. heavy metal contamination
    c. chemical cleaners
    d. chemical building and decorating products
    e. poor quality drinking water
    f. indoor air pollution at home, at school, and at the office

3. **Nervous system allergies to food and/or environmental factors**
   a. some can begin in utero
   b. may go undetected for years
   —The true nature of the condition is often seriously misdiagnosed, often in psychological or psychiatric terms. Once this happens, the condition is from then on inappropriately managed (until appropriate intervention takes place). Symptoms are treated, covered, and suppressed with drugs, but the causes are not identified or corrected, or eliminated.

4. **Increased and repeated use of antibiotics in babies and young children**
   a. kills beneficial intestinal bacteria
   b. promotes overgrowth of harmful yeast organisms (candida) causing many physical and mental symptoms, some of which, are ADD/ADHD

5. **Spinal column misalignments and/or craniosacral system obstructions**
   a. The first cervical vertebra of the spine is often found to be out of alignment in those suffering from ADD/ADHD. In some cases this misalignment occurs at birth.
   b. The craniosacral system consists of the brain, the spinal cord, the bones of the skull and spinal cord, and the protective sheathe that envelops and bathes the brain and spinal cord in a special fluid. An obstruction in this system may complicate or cause ADD/ADHD.

In addition, our TV/Technology culture may *enable* the behavior of ADD/ADHD due to:
   a. mesmerizing, rapid sequence entertainment
   —does not require a person to focus
   b. violent programming
   c. electromagnetic stress
   —due to harmful radiation from the high voltage in the TV tube, especially color sets

With all of these possible contributing factors and others not listed or unknown, it is easy to see why the problem can be so frustrating. It may be even more so for those who are unaware of the multiple causes of ADD/ADHD.

11

Research physicians such as William Crook, M.D., Benjamin Feingold, M.D., Marshall Mandell, M.D., Dr. Doris Rapp, M.D., and C. Orion Truss, M.D., have dedicated their careers to solving the mysteries of ADD and ADHD and other mental-emotional behavioral and physical disorders. Without their work we would know much less about ADD and ADHD than we do now. Each of these trail blazing pioneers has success stories to share about patients whose lives were salvaged from disaster, by making simple changes in the diet and adding nutritional supplements when necessary.

The symptoms of ADD/ADHD are often triggered by environmental factors. Here are some examples of children's writing before, during, and after controlled testing for various allergens and causative chemical substances that are biologically harmful: dust, mold, aerosol disinfectant, school air, and pollen, in that order. These samples are reprinted with permission from Dr. Doris Rapp's book, *Is This Your Child?*

Before Test	*During Test*	*After Test*
Before Test	*During Test*	*After Test*
Before Test	*During Test*	*After Test*

Responses to Food Allergies

Food allergens often provoke similar results to those of environmental allergens. Dr. Mandell offers the following handwriting samples. These show the effects of different foods on the child being tested.

LAURA BELANGER   AGE 7

PRESENTING COMPLAINTS: LEARNING DISABILITIES, LOSS OF EQUILIBRIUM, ENURESIS, INTERMITTENT HYPERACTIVITY AND HYPOACTIVITY

PATIENT'S USUAL PENMANSHIP   *Laura Belanger*

POTATO   PATIENT WAS UNABLE TO REMEMBER HER MIDDLE NAME. SHE EXPERIENCED PHARYNGEAL PAIN AND ABDOMINAL PAIN

Laura Belanger

MILK   PATIENT HICCUPED FREQUENTLY

Vaura el e hger

REVERSAL OF "L" AND "B," OMISSION OF "n"

Jaura Elo langer

REVERSAL OF "L," "B," AND "e"

PEANUT   PATIENT BECAME SILLY WITH UNCONTROLLED LAUGHTER

Laura 'Belanger

13

Children who are having reactions to food and/or environmental allergens run the risk of being labeled ADD or ADHD. Chances are the school nurses, psychologists, and psychiatrists aren't considering all of the possibilities. This is a real tragedy when the solution may be as simple as changing the diet, improving the quality of the indoor air, or discontinuing the use of biologically harmful substances.

Clearing the Air

People may react to chemicals from cleaning and decorating products in an adverse way. In a study, it was determined that school children performed poorly on tests taken early in the morning, following applications of floor cleaners and/or insecticides. As depicted in the illustrations on page 12, behavior and thought processes can be altered by "assaults" from exposure to chemicals and allergens. Eliminating hazardous cleaners and decorating products from your environment is the best way to fix this problem, but this is not always possible.

Installing an air purifier or filtration system in the home, school or office can reduce airborne allergens. Air purifiers clean the air. Mold spores, airborne pathogens, and toxic vapors from cleaning products and building materials are collected and removed. In addition to purifying the air, it is also wise to have the heating/cooling ducts of the building cleaned regularly. This can be done by a professional cleaning company specializing in such things. Unattended to, these heating/cooling ducts can disperse bacteria, dust, and other allergens when the system is turned on.

Personal size air purifiers can protect individuals in their workplace or school. This is especially important as most schools and offices do not budget for duct cleaning or air filtration devices.

Is it Hereditary?

In addition to causes of a dietary or environmental, allergic nature, there are many other possible reasons why a person may have ADD or ADHD. The answer is often different for each individual. The problem is frequently said to be hereditary. This may be due to mineral, enzyme, neurotransmitter, and essential fatty acid, or amino acid deficiencies passed on from one generation to the next rather than to a "bad gene." This is something that can be corrected, nutritionally. "After all, children weren't born with Ritalin in their brains—they certainly don't have a Ritalin deficiency," says Billie Jay Sahley, Ph.D., Executive Director of the Pain & Stress Therapy Center in San Antonio, Texas, and author of *The Natural Way to Control Hyperactivity With Amino Acids and Nutrient Therapy.*.

Critical Thinking

We must be good detectives and gather bits of information. We must learn how to compose the bits of information into meaningful and practical parcels of knowledge. For example, in the 1930's, the government knew that 99 percent of people living at that time were mineral deficient. This information was published in Senate document #264 in the year 1936! Symptoms of mineral deficiency include nervous system dysfunction, memory loss, depression, and mood swings. (see p. 57). The symptoms of mineral deficiency will manifest differently in each individual. Therefore some may have mood swings, or memory loss, or anxiety, and others may not. In some people, mineral deficiencies can manifest as ADD/ADHD, *which is a dysfunction of the central nervous system.* A child who has ADD may have a mother who has mood swings. See how it works? The *mineral deficiency* may be inherited and may manifest differently in the case of each individual. Minerals determine the body's ability to utilize available *amino acids* which, in turn regulate neurotransmitter levels, especially serotonin.

A neurotransmitter is the chemical language sent between cells in the human brain, and neurotransmitters have the responsibility for behavior and learning. A deficiency of neurotransmitters has a dramatic effect on children or adults ability to learn and function in an orderly manner. Dr. Sahley says, "Most children who are hyperactive and A.D.D. are born with a shortage of neurotransmitters, which tends to run in families, mainly on the male side. Hyperactivity and A.D.D. children do not manufacture the needed extra neurotransmitters."

Looking For Clues at the Cellular Level

At this place in our discussion as to "why there is ADD/ADHD," we may actually be at or near to approaching the "heart" of the matter of what ADD and ADHD really are—what really causes the problem . . . for some people. And again we find it is not one answer, but a cascade of answers or clues that lead us closer to a clearer understanding. In the following discussion about causes of ADD/ADHD, the key words are: neurotransmitters, serotonin, B6, protein, tryptophan, amino acids, insulin, calcium, and magnesium.

A Thinking Game

The sentences that follow are pieces of a puzzle. See if you can put the puzzle pieces together into a logical sequence of cause and effect, and, in your own words, come up with an answer that makes sense. You may have to study the sentences and reread them several times, but several conclusions can be drawn from the jumble of facts below.

A neurotransmitter is the chemical language sent between cells in the human brain. Serotonin is a neurotransmitter. People with ADD/ADHD have been shown to improve when serotonin levels are raised. B6 (pyridoxine) is absolutely necessary to form serotonin. Tryptophan is necessary to produce serotonin. Protein supplies dietary free form amino acids *if* the digestive function is sufficient. Many

16

people with ADD/ADHD improve with added protein to their diets. To have enough serotonin, you need enough tryptophan which is essential in its formation. *Kefir* (see p. 37), green food supplements, raw dairy products, bananas, and turkey[1] are excellent sources of tryptophan. Insulin lowers serotonin levels and induces foggy thinking by reducing blood sugar levels to the brain. Calcium releases insulin. Magnesium inhibits the release of insulin. Most children with ADD/ADHD show low magnesium levels at the cellular level, and high calcium.

There are a variety of ways that the above facts may be assembled to tell how the key words interrelate. All of the information we need to solve any problem, exists, somewhere. If we have the clues, we can solve the mysteries. Here is our version of how the above sentences intertwine to tell why you or your child may have ADD/ADHD:

People with ADD/ADHD lack sufficient supplies of neurotransmitters, especially serotonin. Serotonin is manufactured in the brain in the presence of B6 and tryptophan. Tryptophan is an essential amino acid. If tryptophan and B6 are in short supply, the body cannot make serotonin. Therefore, people with ADD/ADHD may require supplements of tryptophan and/or B6. Protein supplies amino acids to the body. If the diet contains sufficient protein and tryptophan rich foods, the supply of amino acids will usually not be a problem. Calcium/magnesium ratio is a key factor, also. Insufficient magnesium can result in high insulin levels which reduces serotonin. Therefore, it is necessary to ensure an adequate supply of magnesium in addition to B6 and amino acids.

---

[1] Some sources say that the heat of cooking destroys tryptophan rendering it useless.

Dr. Sahley has found that most of children she treats have low magnesium levels. With ADD and ADHD, this is often seen in conjunction with poor muscle coordination, a potential indicator of magnesium deficiency.

It's not just mineral deficiencies or amino acid deficiencies, or allergies. It's everything that we are refusing to pay attention to. Like pesticides, for example. It is estimated that by age 5, children in this country consume more pesticides than is considered safe for an entire lifetime. 50 years ago, the word "diet" referred to "food." Clean air and pure water were readily available then. They were as important as food, but taken for granted. What about now?

If you participated in the "thinking game" exercise above, you used deductive reasoning skills to draw your own conclusions from the available facts. This is what scientists do. Perhaps this is what the scientists did who invented Ritalin as a treatment for ADD/ADHD. Perhaps these scientists knew that people with ADD or ADHD often have low serotonin levels in their brain, so they invented Ritalin. Ritalin raises the serotonin levels in the brain and this is helpful for those with ADD/ADHD. Unfortunately, Ritalin does this in a way that stresses the body out even more than it was stressed out to begin with, and may cause many undesirable side effects as well. Therefore Ritalin is not necessarily *bad*, it just may cause more problems than it solves. In cases where Ritalin "works", it appears to be a miracle treatment. That is probably one of the reasons doctors continue to prescribe it.

ADD/ADHD are not mysterious diseases of unknown origin any longer. Children and adults are being successfully treated through natural means. It is the indiscriminate use of behavior modifying drugs that should be examined. We need to ask questions about the long term consequences. The causes vary and are often different in each individual.

Chapter 4

The First Step
Toward Changing Your Diet

The first step toward changing your diet is to list the foods you eat often or daily, and begin to notice which foods are craved. If it is your child who has the ADD or ADHD, what are his or her favorite foods? Are there foods that he or she loves? Do some foods somehow make you feel better? These are often the culprits. Write these down. Make a list **on paper**.

Foods that people crave are often the foods causing them the most problems.

According to Dr. Marshall Mandell, addictive food allergies are very common and cause an amazing variety of chronic physical and mental symptoms/disorders in millions of people. Physicians often do not recognize the underlying nature of their ailments and incorrectly blame "stress," viruses, spouses, employers, jobs, ADD/ADHD, etc.

In an article in *Medical World News*, January 30, 1970, Dr. Mandell stated that a person can become addicted to foods and the addicting foods can produce physical and mental withdrawal symptoms. These symptoms can manifest themselves as an allergic attack - the same as the "narcotic addict's withdrawal symptoms that demand another "fix" for relief, and the alcoholic's DT syndrome that demands another drink."

Mandell tells the story of a 33-year-old female patient who was extremely hostile and emotionally upset upon arrival at the clinic. "Shortly after the visit began, she decided she would not stay in the doctor's office another minute, saying she was going to have a chocolate bar on the way home—that she had to have one immediately." Dr. Mandell was able to persuade the woman to stay a little longer, long enough for him to test her for chocolate sensitivity. "Within a few minutes, she became very warm and then had chills. Her speech became slurred, and she was acutely anxious and confused." A symptom relieving dose of chocolate—the addicting allergen—was given, and "within twenty minutes she was smiling, amazed that she actually felt cheerful."

Dr. R. Glen Green, M.D., C.M. in a paper presented at the Second Annual Conference of the Canadian Association for Children with Learning Disabilities, October 1979, says: "My cardinal rule is 'if you crave it, don't eat it.' I don't care whether it is bread or beans, Tang or coffee, milk or mustard, ketchup or cauliflower. This dictum is irrefutable. To be addicted is to be allergic."

Green likens the stages of this process to that of an addiction to nicotine. The first cigarette may make you feel ill and dizzy and sick, but once you become adapted to the nicotine, a state of addiction develops. Once this happens, the addiction creates uncomfortable symptoms that can only be alleviated by having *another* cigarette, and another, and another. The addictive cycle may repeat itself day after day for years.

Look For Connections

Dr. Doris Rapp and Dr. Marshall Mandell have done extensive work with children regarding food allergies and environmental sensitivities. Dr. Rapp says that parents and others must begin to look for connections because behavior is so often linked to food and/or environmental allergens.

Dr. Rapp always asks parents to pay attention to symptoms that may be related, *". . . For example, are dark eye circles noticed in relation to your child's temper outbursts and inability to speak clearly? Do the red ears, headaches and inability to write or draw all occur at the same time?"* By paying attention to these things, *"You may be able to recognize that certain physical changes in your child's appearance provide warning signals . . . and if you can spot the early clues, you may be able to prevent many problems and make your family life much less stressful."*

Taking the First Step

We may begin this first step of observation immediately. There are at least two ways to do this:

1. Keep a food diary for one week. Write down absolutely everything you, (or your child), eats. Also write down how you feel emotionally, mentally, and physically throughout the day, and make appropriate notes concerning your child.

2. Record all cravings for food, candy, and beverages. Rate the craving on a scale from 1-10. Ten means you cannot live without it. One means you could easily pass it up.

Dr. Rapp suggests that if you want to learn even more about what effects various foods may have, do the following. If you suspect a certain frequently eaten food of causing a problem, feed that food to your child and have your child:

1. Write and draw. Does either change before and 20 to 60 minutes after a food is eaten? If it does, the items ingested could affect your child's school work.

2. Take the pulse. If it increases by 20 to 40 points after eating a particular food, once again your child's body could be warning you about some food sensitivity.

3. Use a Pocket Peak Flow Meter if your child has asthma. Use this before and 20 minutes after each food. If the reading on the gauge falls 15%, or 50 or so points, that beverage or food could be the cause of wheezing.

The Real First Step

The real first step toward changing a possible symptom evoking diet is *deciding to*. Turning your attention toward what you want is necessary. What makes anyone decide to do anything? Usually they have a reason. You will need a reason, also. Your decision to do something about the problem of ADD/ADHD depends on it. Once you have a reason, and you decide that you want to do something different, all that is left is to discover *how* you will go about it. We can help you with the how part, but you have to help yourself with the why.

Why do you want to change, heal, or alleviate the symptoms of ADD or ADHD? This may sound like a silly question, but it is important to be specific. If the answer is an "obvious" one, then simply state it. If the answer is not immediately obvious, then perhaps it is not such a silly question after all. If you think that nothing can be done about it, then that says something, too. What could the result be for your child if you are wrong? Why do you want to change, heal, or alleviate the symptoms of ADD or ADHD? Be specific when you answer this question, because the answer you give will become your *reason*. And your REASON will become your driving force when the going gets tough.

You may have to remind yourself once or twice a day, why you are going to incredible lengths to feed your child or yourself differently or to figure out which supplements work best in your individual situation. The process of changing or of healing is not always easy. It may take some time. There are old habits to overcome, and new knowledge to acquire. If your reason for wanting to make these changes is specific enough, it will help you remain focused on your goal and encourage you to keep going until you have achieved what you set out to achieve. The results will be worth it. Right now would be a good time for you to answer the "why" question. It is best if you write the answer down. You may use the space below.

Why I want to change, heal, or alleviate the symptoms of ADD/ADHD in myself or my child:

If you don't have a reason you'll need to get one. Because, if you know what you want, (goals), and you have a reason that motivates you, you're halfway there. So what are you waiting for? Get a reason!

Chapter 5

What Should You Eat?

Are you looking for a magic diet? A quick and easy plan that will change things overnight and make the ADD or ADHD go away and never come back? We wish we could help you.

Unfortunately, it is difficult to say, "This is the right diet for an individual, and that is the wrong one." What is needed, in many cases, is an individualized diet based on a cause and effect investigation of person specific sensitivities. The question of what to eat can be answered by beginning with a list of what not to eat. This cannot, however, work for everybody, because some people will be allergic to oranges, for example, or rice. The answer you finally arrive at will be an individual one.

It is a journey, and as long as you don't quit, you will find the answers you are looking for. However, a carefully followed diet consisting of single-food meals eaten in a rotary manner—a rotary diversified diet—will frequently provide the information about tolerated and offending foods in each individual case. The same diet can be followed by many individuals for diagnostic purposes.

This book is designed to help you. One thing we hope you understand as a result of reading this book is that the management of ADD/ADHD will vary as much as the people who have it. However, the *basics* stay the same: an allergy free diet, appropriate supplementation, helpful non-dietary approaches, detoxification, and some form of aerobic exercise (no details about exercise will be included in this book).

The journey for some is longer and more difficult than it is for others. Many people who were "cured" of ADD/ADHD, simply removed milk from their diets. It was that easy. They were lucky. It's not always this simple.

Dr. Lendon Smith, M.D., of Portland, Oregon, stated in an article in *Health Counselor* magazine[2] that he has concluded that between 50 to 70 percent of the American childhood population is allergic to cow's milk and dairy products. "All I have to do in this case is stop the milk and the problem clears up," said Dr. Smith, who also noted that cravings for dairy products can indicate a calcium deficiency. Billie Jay Sahley, Ph.D., says, "A child who is found to be food sensitive to dairy products is not likely to be receiving proper amounts of dietary calcium or tryptophan." She also finds at least 50 percent of the children she tests to be sensitive to dairy products. "Yet," she says, "Dairy products are a major food source of tryptophan. So if the child's diet is restricted from all dairy products, he should be given these vital nutrients in supplement form."

Not to confuse you, but to demonstrate our point about how this really is a process of discovery—others have found that *adding* milk—*raw* milk—to the diet of some individuals, is all it has taken to relieve their ADD/ADHD. One of the reasons given for the success of this method is that the raw protein supplies a generous helping of amino acids, including, and especially, tryptophan. Tryptophan is an essential amino acid that is necessary for the brain to be able to produce serotonin, which helps to relieve the symptoms of ADD/ADHD. (see pp. 16-17).

Unfortunately, the availability of fresh raw cow's milk is limited by state jurisdiction. Raw organic goat's milk may be easier to obtain and is just as good, if not better.

---

[2] (vol.6, no.1) "Attention Deficit Hyperactivity Disorder—Focusing on Alternative Treatments"

Dr. Bernard Jensen states, *"Mother Nature has provided us with one of her most nourishing foods available to us, goat's milk. Exceptionally high in protein and an excellent source of absorbable calcium/magnesium. I used it on my health ranch for many years in order to recuperate myself and then my patients."*

Others have found it necessary to also remove sweeteners from the diet as in the following case:

As a parent I watched my daughter go from a hyperactive, defiant child to blossom as a beautiful "normal" child—a simple change of eliminating sweeteners along with no milk and adding a few supplements.

At age 13 she went from a "D" average to a straight "A" student, from a fourth grade reading level to reading on an 11.8 reading level by changing diet and adding some vitamin C, calcium, magnesium, zinc, and Kyolic garlic capsules.— Jo-Anne Rohn-Cook.

It is possible that our children are predisposed to allergies because of the way we feed them when they are infants. As a normal occurrence, babies are born with leaky gut (food particles passing through the intestinal wall into the blood stream). If rice, wheat or cow's milk is given to them at an early age, this may cause food allergies that surface as they grow older.

So what is the answer? There is no one answer. We are presenting you with the latest information. You get to play detective. It's a great adventure. Of course there *are* some basics.

Are You Ready For This?

So you really want to know what you should eat? Okay, here goes. *Our sources say that you should eat a diet consisting of natural, "organic" foods. As a general rule of thumb, supplement the diet with digestive enzymes,* *electrolyte trace minerals, and essential fatty acids. Plus any nutrients, herbs, homeopathic remedies, etc., specific to your condition or that your physician has recommended for you. People with ADHD should limit their fruit intake due to problems at the cellular level with low blood sugar (hypoglycemia). (See p.36). Both groups (ADD & ADHD) require high protein. Simple carbohydrates (white flour, for example) should be avoided. Avoid all foods with artificial additives, chemical dyes, and preservatives. Avoid all foods that provoke an allergic reaction. Use "really" raw honey or stevia powder for a sweetener. Eat as many raw foods as possible. Drink pure water. Breathe clean air.*

That's it in a nutshell. Are you motivated? Not if you weren't already. That's because a list won't get you to change anything. That's why we spent so much time in other chapters talking about goals and reasons. You need those things.

Find Out What Foods are Causing a Problem

ADD and ADHD have been successfully treated by alternative methods for over two decades now. Changing the diet can definitely help in most cases. To find out what foods are causing the problem, it may be necessary to do one or more of the following:

1. fast and then eat foods separately to notice their effect
2. use a rotation diet
3. get tested for allergies
4. read about what other people did
5. practice proper food combining
6. see a doctor who specializes in natural care for ADD/ADHD

You may want to start by choosing an approach that appeals to you the most. Some people prefer visiting a doctor and having tests done. Others prefer a do-it-yourself at home approach using single food testing and following it with an elimination diet avoiding proven offenders, or multiple food elimination tests, or over the counter supplements. It's your choice.

Feingold, a Pioneer

Dr. Benjamin Feingold was the first to popularize a special diet for kids with hyperactivity and aggressive behavior. The Feingold diet originally presented in *Why Your Child is Hyperactive* is still used by some today. This diet prohibits the intake of synthetic (artificial) colors, flavors, and preservatives, and all foods containing natural salicylates[3] including:

> almonds, apples (also cider & cider vinegar), apricots, all berries, cherries, cloves, coffee, cucumbers and pickles, currants, grapes and raisins (also wine & wine vinegar), nectarines, oil of wintergreen (methyl salicylate), oranges, peaches, peppers (bell & chilies), plums and prunes, tangerines, tea, tomatoes, potatoes, and eggplant.

Dr. Feingold is to be highly congratulated. He was there with the answers for some parents when no one else seemed to care what happened to these children. The Feingold Program has helped many people.

"I'm no good at all," proclaimed seven year old Jacob. Besides poor self esteem, Jacob cried easily and suffered from insomnia, frequent headaches and stomach aches. His behavior at school, at home, and in public was becoming increasingly disruptive. His first grade teacher repeatedly banished him behind an isolation screen because he couldn't sit still, be quiet, or keep his hands to himself. At home, he was increasingly unmanageable: noisy, argumentative, impulsive, forgetful, overactive, and unable to follow directions.

---

[3] He noted that yellow #5 caused symptoms in some children and noted that some of them reacted to aspirin which is a salicylate compound, BUT each food coloring has a different chemical structure and a child might react to some, not necessarily all of the salicylate foods.

29

His mother stumbled across an address for the Feingold Association. After looking at a sample newsletter which contained children's artwork of how they felt before and after the Feingold Program, Jacob declared, "I want to do that diet." They followed the Feingold instructions meticulously, and within a week Jacob was transformed. His physical complaints were gone and his teacher commented that he had suddenly become a classroom asset. Jacob is now in the gifted and talented program.

* * *

Stuart, age 32, had been plagued throughout his life by stomach problems, headaches, anxiety, fatigue, and irritability, symptoms frequently associated with ADD/ADHD. He felt lousy—was bouncing off the walls, and under pressure but couldn't concentrate. After years of eating junk food, he began the Fiengold Program. The results were immediate. "I can go through a day and the pressure doesn't bother me. I'm stronger with more vitality and more stamina. It has helped me at work and it has helped my relationship with my son."

"Well it Doesn't work for Everyone"

Unfortunately, the Feingold Plan has suffered harsh criticism since its early days for not being effective *all* of the time. There are a number of possible reasons for its failure in some cases. Perhaps there was an allergy to foods that were *permitted* on the diet such as corn, wheat, eggs, or chicken. Perhaps there was a mineral deficiency, or a spinal misalignment. Perhaps the instructions were not correctly followed. Perhaps, as Dr. Mandell says, "It simply is not comprehensive enough to meet the needs of all individuals who suffer from ADD/ADHD, but it was, and still is, an important contribution to medical history."

Remember, you are the detective becoming the expert on the health of you and your family.

Could Yeast be Your Problem?

Dr. C. Orian Truss, M.D., was another pioneer in the realm of dietary related behavior problems. Truss did original research on *candida albicans*, the yeast organism that lives in everyone and causes problems for some. Candida, as it is commonly referred to, could be a problem that complicates or *causes* ADD/ADHD.

The candida yeast can be a trouble maker. It is not to be confused with *nutritional yeast*, a food supplement. Nutritional yeast is good.

How Does Candida Become a Problem?

Candida becomes a problem when it overpopulates the intestinal, vaginal, and/or respiratory tracts. This happens as the result of repeated rounds of antibiotics, prolonged stress, and poor diet. Antibiotics kill off the good intestinal flora, giving candida more room to grow. Eating foods such as freshly made sauerkraut, miso, and plain yogurt containing "live" cultures (available at the health food store) replenish the "friendly" bacteria we need to be healthy. Eaten on a regular basis, these foods will contribute to good health.

The "good" flora include, but are not limited to: Bifidobacteria, L. Acidophilus, L. Rhamnosus, and L. Salivarius. These microorganisms constitute an integral part of the healthy gastrointestinal ecology.

Candida organisms **love** sugar, fermented foods, refined carbohydrates, and molds (nuts often contain molds we are unaware of, unless the nuts are absolutely fresh, meaning right off the tree). You may know someone who has been on a "yeast free" diet. Candida may be a problem for you or your child. You may need to go on a special diet that would eliminate:

fruit, dried fruit, nuts, all processed foods and white flour products, leavened bread, all fermented foods except for miso,

31

all sweeteners, soft drinks, fruit juice, pasta and all dairy products except for raw milk and "live" yogurt or kefir

In addition to this special diet, you may need to take anti-candida medication and allergy treatments, depending on the severity of the situation. It may also be beneficial to take a probiotic supplement of various acidophilus and bifidus cultures. Many people with ADD/ADHD benefit from probiotic supplements (acidophilus and bifidus) whether or not they have an obvious candida problem.

In *The Missing Diagnosis*, Dr. Truss explains that the symptoms of candida overgrowth are often mistaken for psychological or psychiatric disorders. "They may say you're neurotic," he says, "but do you experience: depression, anxiety, irrational irritability . . . loss of self confidence, inability to cope, lethargy, symptoms from contact with foods and chemical odors, and in addition, in children, hyperactivity, irritability, learning problems, recurrent ear infections . . . poor appetite, erratic sleep patterns?"

Sounds like ADD/ADHD doesn't it? It could be, because candida is an important factor in some cases of ADD/ADHD. To find out, you have to experiment a little with different approaches. If you are persistent you will find what works best, and you *will* have an answer and life *will* get better.

Many people are working now to get this information to you. Soon alternative methods of treating ADD/ADHD will become common knowledge.

The Leaders
Dr. Robert Mendehlsohn, M.D., pediatrician, was among the first of the medical practitioners of this century to become famous for his message that medicine should be given back into the hands of the people. He advised us to become our own best expert concerning our health and well

being and that of our family. Dr. Mendehlsohn wrote several books. To learn more about ADD and ADHD, read *How to Raise a Healthy Child in Spite of Your Doctor.*

Doris Rapp, M.D., lecturer, author, professor, environmental medical specialist and pediatric allergist in Buffalo, NY, has taken a powerful stand regarding the connection between food allergies and ADD/ADHD. Her research is so thorough and well documented it boggles ones mind to think that there are any children at all left on prescription drugs when such excellent alternatives exist. Read *Is This Your Child?* and *Is This Your Child's World?*

Dr. William Crook has written numerous books and articles on the subject and has helped thousands of people. See *Help For the Hyperactive Child* and *Solving the Puzzle of Your Hard-to-Raise Child.*

Mary Ann Block, D.O., is author, lecturer, and medical director of the Block Center. The Block center is a medical facility in the Dallas/Fort Worth Area for adults and children with chronic health problems. Dr. Block stresses the importance of a healthy digestive tract and teaches people to rebuild their health from the inside out. Read *No More Ritalin: Treating ADHD without Drugs.*

Marshall Mandell, M.D., retired physician, author, lecturer, and former medical director of the New England Foundation for Allergy and Environmental Diseases has spent the better portion of his life teaching people how to overcome food, pollen, mold, and chemical allergies. He has shown how conditions such as arthritis, colitis, headaches, chronic fatigue, many cases of schizophrenia, cerebral palsy, multiple sclerosis, learning disabilities, and hyperactivity can clear up quickly when the offending food is removed from the diet and/or when airborne allergens are treated and environmental and dietary chemicals are controlled or eliminated. Read *Dr. Mandell's 5-Day Allergy Relief System.*

Billie Jay Sahley, Ph.D., Jeffrey Bland, Ph.D., Dr. Edward Howell, and the late Dr. Carl Pfieffer, M.D. These are some of the many dedicated people who care about what you are going through. And you will find that the greater your commitment to finding the answers you seek, the more help will come your way.

So what should you eat as you start your self-help program? Really it's back to the list on page 27-28. We made light of giving you a list to follow, but in reality, this list is an excellent place to start. It may offer just the information that you need to assure a healthy life for you and your children.

Do it Yourself at Home

As far as discovering what individual foods may be causing your or your child's problems, you can do a Single Food Elimination Diet[4] at home. The diet consists of giving regularly eaten foods *two or more times a week,* only once every five to seven days. This means that if milk is taken on Tuesday, it is not to be taken again until Sunday, Monday, or Tuesday. On the chosen test day, after the person has not eaten *anything* for 3-5 hours, *only* milk and cottage cheese are given and the effect they have upon the person is noted. If there is going to be a reaction, it will usually happen within 15 minutes to an hour. A rash, muscle or joint pains, may take up to 24 hours to appear (by then you may not be able to link it to the milk if other foods have been eaten.) The instructions again, are as follows:

1. Test one food at a time.
2. Eat the food one day and then wait *five to seven days* before eating it again.
3. The fifth, sixth, or seventh day is testing day.
4. On testing day, eat nothing for the first 3-5 hours after waking. Then eat only the food you are

---

[4] For more detailed information, refer to Dr. Marshall Mandell's self-help books, and *Is This Your Child?* by Doris Rapp, M.D.,

testing for. If you are testing for more than one food a day, you should wait 3-5 hours between foods and have only one food at each meal—the food you are testing for.

5. Note any and all reactions. Write everything down on paper.

You can do this with twenty one different foods a week, eating a different food for each of the three meals each day. You will soon learn which foods cause problems.

Common dietary allergens are:

wheat, corn, rice, oat, peas, soy, peanuts, milk, artificial colors, pure baker's chocolate, eggs, cane sugar, chicken, beef, pork, tomato, potato, orange, lettuce, broccoli, green beans, coffee, cheese, and alcohol

The major disadvantage of the Single Food Diet is that it may provide only a partial picture. Symptoms from removing an offending food may get worse for 2 or 3 days following the removal of that food from the diet. This is due to the allergic addictive withdrawal syndrome similar to a "nicotine fit" when a smoker gives up smoking. Also, the person being tested may be "cheating" by eating other offending foods during the test time. This may affect the accuracy of the results.

This is where some people have become frustrated and given up. "We took away milk, we took away corn, wheat, sugar—nothing worked." This is because the person being tested was reacting to other foods in the diet. We never said it would be easy. Repeated efforts will help you to understand more. See a professional if you feel you need extra help in determining the foods that cause a reaction in you or the person you care about. Success will result when the commitment overrides the difficulty of the situation.

More on What to Eat

Laurene B. Procaccini, RN and Orthomolecular Consultant at Bio-Spectrum Analysis, Inc. points out that there is a biochemical difference between ADD and ADHD. The difference is the hyperactivity part, and she is able to see this difference, consistently, on a cellular level. She believes that ADHD people are "fast oxidizers" who are often "high strung" or "emotional." This person, she says, "should not have any sweets, simple carbohydrates, fruits, or fruit juice." Instead, proteins, *raw* dairy, vegetables, and fats (butter, avocado, sour cream—organic, please) are required. These foods help to eliminate blood sugar disturbances at the cellular level resulting in erratic behavior and mood swings.

Blood sugar abnormalities are often unable to be detected by physicians treating those with ADD/ADHD. The reason is that the doctors are looking at the blood, not the cells of other tissue. Unfortunately, the American diet, high in refined sugars, additives, and preservatives, exacerbates the problem. Hyperactive behavior may result when blood sugar levels rise rapidly after the intake of these foods. When the blood sugar levels are high, the body releases insulin. This radically *lowers* the blood sugar. This drop in blood sugar then forces the body to produce adrenaline. The result is hyperkinetic behavior, mental confusion, irritability, anxiety, nervousness, and violence.

The "slow oxidizer" on the other hand, is the person with ADD without the hyperactivity. This person's body doesn't metabolize available glucose fast enough (as opposed to a sudden rise in the blood sugar of the "fast oxidizer") This person is prone to confusion, nervousness, irritability, and panic. "The [diet] for the slow oxidizer consists of protein 3 times daily, a good quality complex carbohydrate (no white flour), vegetables, and one piece of juicy fruit per day," says Procaccini.

People with ADD/ADHD require protein snacks throughout the day. Raw protein is preferable. *Sprouted* soy powder and a high quality green foods supplement (see p. 65) can provide additional dietary protein. These supplements are convenient, as they can be quickly mixed into a special drink or "shake." If pure, raw honey is tolerated, the drink may be lightly sweetened.

Your new diet will help you get healthy from the inside out. However, *the nutritional value of any food depends upon its absorption in the intestinal tract.* Therefore, **no matter how great your diet, you have to have healthy insides to gain the benefits of that food.**

Studies at the Block Center in Dallas/Fort Worth, TX, showed that 95 percent of people studied had too much yeast (candida albicans) in their intestines, another 50 percent had harmful bacteria, and approximately 25 percent had parasites. To remedy this problem, Dr. Block recommends a variety of treatments including proper diet and supplementation with lactobacillus acidophilus and bifidobacterium infantis in order to recolonize beneficial intestinal bacteria.

Having healthy insides means having thriving colonies of "friendly" bacteria populating the intestines. Friendly bacteria keeps the colon working properly, discourages parasites, and contributes to proper digestion.

A way of getting high quality protein and recolonizing the intestines with beneficial organisms at the same time is to eat *kefir*.

Kefir is a cultured and enzyme-rich food made from milk, that is chock full of friendly micro-organisms which help restore the inner ecology. Kefir contains *complete* protein with all the essential amino acids. Kefir also provides abundant calcium and magnesium, tryptophan, and several essential B vitamins. Because the body converts tryptophan into serotonin, an important chemical neurotransmitter, some people call Kefir "Nature's tranquilizer" or "Nature's Prozac." Even people who are lactose (milk) intolerant are able to eat kefir. The only drawback is that to get a good supply you may have to make it yourself. Luckily it's easy to do. Find out how by reading *The Magic of Kefir* by Donna Gates with Linda Schatz. Also, ask about ordering kefir at your local health food store.

Another great source of protein is soy. However, soy products may contain naturally occuring enzyme inhibitors that may be less than beneficial to humans. Fermented or sprouted soy foods are fine. These would include miso, tempeh, natto, shoyu, and sprouted soy products. According to Sally Fallon and nutritionist Mary Enig, Ph.D., harmful digestive enzyme inhibitors contained in the unfermented bean, normally prohibit soy from being digested, (such as found in soy products like tofu, soy milk, and soy cheese). Digestive enzyme inhibitors may create an overworked pancreas and also may interfere with protein digestion. Fermented and sprouted soy forms have converted the digestive enzyme inhibitors, thereby allowing for proper digestion and the assimilation of nutrients.[5] Trypsin inhibitors, also found in unfermented soy, are growth depressants that may restrict the normal development of children's bodies. Therefore to gain the benefits of soy, choose only fermented or sprouted soy foods.

Every step you take toward treating ADD/ADHD naturally is a step toward regaining balance. Balance on the inside, balance on the outside, balance in your everyday life. Your investigation of alternative treatments for ADD/ADHD shows your desire to do so and for that you are to be congratulated for having an intelligent approach to these problems.

---

[5] *Digestive* enzymes inhibitors are different from the beneficial *protease* inhibitors found in soy, which have been shown to be beneficial in fighting cancer.

So, what should you eat? Well, if we took the basic food recommendations of the experts and created a simple chart it would look something like this:

	ADD	**ADHD**
protein	more of	more of
starch	moderate	less of
vegetables	more of	more of
fruits	some	little to none
fats	more of	more of
oils	some	some
sugars	individual	individual

In **addition**, there would be instructions for *when* to eat certain foods and *how*. These instructions are collectively referred to as "food combining." This may be one of the most difficult of all dietary practices to observe, but the results are worth it. The objective is to eat foods that are digested quickly separate from foods that take longer to digest. For example, proteins and starches—meat and potatoes—don't mix. They require different digestive enzymes in addition to varying lengths of time for complete digestion to take place. If a food that digests quickly is eaten with a food that does not—fruit and meat, for example—the result may be bloating and gas. Eating this way consistently promotes maldigestion, thereby cultivating an environment for disease.

Fruit digests rather quickly and should be eaten alone allowing 30 minutes to elapse before other foods are eaten. Melon should be *completely* isolated from any other food or fruit and also given 30 minutes. Proteins should not be eaten with starch, but fats may. Therefore you can still have sour cream on your baked potato. And *low starch* or *non-starch* vegetables can go with any foods. Sugar snacks (if tolerated) should be eaten alone on an empty stomach. A natural alternative to refined sugar is stevia. It may help to balance blood sugar and control sugar cravings. Pure, *totally unprocessed* honey is also very good, and is a natural source of raw protein and amino acids.

A simple chart for food combining would look like this:

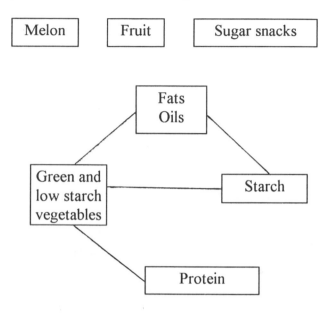

And here are the food classifications in case you were wondering:

Proteins: nuts, seeds, peanuts, lentils, milk, cheese, eggs, flesh foods, sunflower sprouts, sprouted soy, chlorella, wheat and barley grass, green supplements
Starch: potatoes, yams, winter squash, carrots, beets, dry beans, cereals, grains, bread
Fats: avocados, vegetable oil, butter, cream, margarine, lard
Low starch vegetables: celery, sweet corn, peas, broccoli, sweet pepper, summer squash, parsley, eggplant, alfalfa sprouts, mushrooms, green beans, onion, lettuce, spinach, cucumber, cauliflower, cabbage, collards, bok choy, radish, kale, asparagus, garlic

Fruit: tomato, kiwi, strawberry, pineapple, lemon, lime, citrus fruits, banana, date, grapes, dried fruits, berries, pears, apple, peach, cherry, papaya
Melon: watermelon, honeydew, cantaloupe, casaba, crenshaw, muskmellon
Sugars: white sugar, brown sugar, raw sugar, honey, cane syrup, maple

Blood tests are available that can tell you what foods and food combinations will never work for your particular metabolic type. The tests tell you which foods and food combinations your body lacks the enzyme to digest. Information on the Food Intolerance Test is available by contacting Jared Deff, N.D. in Portland, OR.. You can also request through your local medical doctor or naturopath, an IGG (immunoglobin G) Test (Great Smokies Lab, Ashville, N.C.) for allergies and immune weakness. Knowing *exactly* which foods or food combinations you should avoid may be helpful. The mother in the following story would not have guessed that potatoes had been causing a problem for her daughter.

I would have never thought that potatoes could have been causing extreme fits of screaming and what appeared to be pain or rage in my one year old daughter. Emily was having recurrent ear infections from age 6 weeks and had been treated with round after round of antibiotic causing a candida problem in addition to the ear infections. She had diarrhea, candida, colic, tonsillitis, ear infections, and insomnia. At around age 6 months I took her off all antibiotics and visited a homeopathic doctor. The homeopathic remedies cured the ear infection up right away. In addition, we both followed a yeast free diet and took extra EFA's. Because she had been so ill, it took about two years of eating differently to get her well enough that she wouldn't react to any foods, although she still is not supposed to eat potato or fruit and sugar in combination. Now she is 8 years old and can't remember ever being sick. She may have ended up having ADD if we

41

hadn't done something right away. The Food Intolerance Test provided the missing pieces of the puzzle. What a relief! —R.B.

Maintaining Acid/Alkaline Balance

No matter which "diet" you choose to follow, it is important to pay attention to the acid/alkaline balance of your body.

Acid/alkaline balance refers to the pH of your body's internal environment measurable through bodily fluids: blood, urine, and saliva. pH is only a number. You needn't understand scientific principles to apply this information. Blood pH is 7.4 (when healthy). Urine pH—optimally—is 6.2; saliva, 6.8.

Our diets and lifestyles often keep us in the more acidic range of pH creating fatigue and lowered immunity. In addition, acidity creates the perfect environment for parasites, candida, harmful bacteria, and cancer.

The objective is to keep a good balance, eating enough of each to retain optimum health. Here is a quick reference chart for common foods:

Alkaline Forming Foods: (75% of your diet)
vegetables
potato, squash, parsnips
grains: millet, buckwheat, corn, sprouted grains
fruits: most fruits especially sweet ones
nuts: almonds, brazil nuts, sprouted seeds
beans: soy, lima, sprouted beans
oils: olive, soy, sesame, sunflower, corn, safflower

Acid Forming Foods: (25% of your diet)
meat, fowl, fish
dairy products
grains: rice, barley, wheat, oats, rye
fruits: sour fruits, strawberries, cranberries

nuts: all others except above
beans: lentil, navy, aduki, kidney
oils: nut oils, butter
sugars

On a Daily Basis

If you want to determine whether you are acid or alkaline,
it's easy, if you have a roll of pH testing paper. Just take a
urine sample first thing in the morning and you will be able
to see right away, if you ate the proper foods yesterday.
This will give you an indication of what you have to eat
today to balance yourself...but don't forget your food
combining at the same time. As a general rule of thumb eat
75 percent alkaline forming foods and 25 percent acid
forming to keep a healthy balance.

Stress, worry, and incessant activity also create
acidity. Therefore, lifestyle is just as important as food in
maintaining acid/alkaline balance. Deep breathing is very
healthful and beneficial in all aspects of one's life. Massage
will help to relieve stress.

What Not to Eat

What is in your food, that can play havoc in your body and
aggravate your symptoms? BHT/BHA, Ethoxyquin,
Artificial color, Propylene Glycol, Sodium Nitrite, EDTA,
MSG, Nutrasweet, and Polyvinyl chloride, for starters.
These are chemical or artificially manufactured substances
that should be avoided. Over 2,000 additives are used in
food to make it look prettier, taste better, last longer on the
shelves and save manufacturers money. Many of these
harmful food additives can trigger behavioral problems or
cause immune system breakdown, further complicating
proper diagnosis of the reasons behind ADD/ADHD.

BHT/BHA. These petroleum products are used to stabilize
fats in foods. In the process of metabolizing BHA and
BHT, chemical changes occur in the body. These changes
have been reported to cause reduced growth rate in animal

studies and the inhibition of white blood cell stimulation which may put the immune system in jeopardy. In humans, BHT/BHA may cause skin blisters, hemorrhaging of the eye, weakness, discomfort in breathing, cancer and the reduction of the body's own antioxidant enzyme, glutathione peroxidase.

Artificial Color. Approximately 95% of the synthetic colorings used in the U.S. are coal tar derivatives. Red #40 is a possible carcinogen. Yellow #6, causes increased susceptibility to fatal viruses in animals. Dyes are stored by the body tissues for a long time and are difficult to remove.

Propylene Glycol. Used as a de-icing fluid for airplanes, this chemical is added to food and skin products to maintain texture and moisture as well as inhibiting bacteria growth in the product. This additive inhibits the growth of "friendly" bacteria in your intestines and decreases the amount of moisture in the intestinal tract possibly leading to constipation and diseases of the colon.

Sodium Nitrite. Used in the curing of meats, this substance participates in a chemical reaction in the body that may become carcinogenic.

EDTA. This substance is used to prevent fat and oil products from going rancid and also keeps fruits and vegetables from turning brown. When present in excess it can cause kidney damage and calcium imbalance. Excess EDTA can also mimic certain vitamin deficiencies.

MSG. Most people are aware of the possible dangers of MSG and request it be withheld from restaurant foods. MSG has been found to damage the retina of infant rats, and destroy nerve cells of an area of the brain known as the hypothalamus. Some humans who react to MSG exhibit headaches, tightness in the chest and burning sensations in the extremities. Hidden sources of MSG can be Hydrolyzed

Protein, Sodium Caseinate or Calcium Caseinate, Autolyzed Yeast or Yeast Extract and Gelatin.

Nutrasweet (aspartame). This popular sugar substitute may have very adverse effects on the human body. It has been reported to cause recurrent headaches, mental aberrations, seizures, suicidal tendencies, behavioral disorders, birth defects, skin lesions and urinary bladder disturbances. The Nutrasweet "hangover" may consist of malaise, nausea, headaches, dizziness, visual disturbances and convulsions. Since people with ADD/ADHD may exhibit many of these symptoms, this additive should absolutely be eliminated from their diet.

Insecticides and Pesticides. A must to maintaining a healthy diet, is to avoid pesticides and insecticides. These hazards are found just about everywhere. Home pesticides are no less lethal than those used in agriculture. They are altering our biological condition, producing animal and bird mutations, and contributing to the demise of the planet. Pesticides may trigger behavioral problems in people with chemical sensitivities, and may directly affect the central nervous system. A list of fruits and vegetables that are most susceptible to contamination from pesticides, (in order of highest risk of contamination), are...strawberries, bell peppers, (green and red), spinach, cherries, peaches, cantaloupe, (from Mexico), celery, apples, apricots, green beans, grapes, and cucumbers. Use organic foods instead.

Live Long and Prosper
The question of what to eat is best answered individually. Basically we want you to eat "real" foods in as close to their natural state as possible—minus the ones you have found to adversely affect you. We want you and your children to be well and live a long and healthy life. The food you eat, and everything else you take into your body, including thoughts, plays a part in that. Take stock of what's important. Reconsider your priorities. Breathe.

Chapter 6

Tasty Recipes

Fairly simple recipes, in no particular order. Common food allergens can be avoided and yet the food still tastes good! If you are switching from commercial produce to organic, you may find that the food tastes better. You will be able to use less salt and other seasonings because the food has a delicious flavor of its own.

CANNELLINI BEAN DIP
1 clove garlic
4 cups cooked cannellini beans, drained
1 cup fresh basil leaves
3 Tbsp. fresh lemon juice
1/2 tsp. salt
1/4 tsp. fresh ground pepper
Put all in food processor and process until smooth. Serve as dip for raw vegetables or (wheat free) crackers

RAW VEGETABLES FOR DIP
carrot sticks
cauliflower, cut small
celery, cut small
summer squash, sliced or cut into sticks
broccoli, cut small
rutabaga
radish slices
fennel, cut small

KALE WITH GINGER
1 bunches fresh kale
1/2 inch (or to taste) chunk fresh ginger root
1/2 cup water
Wash kale. Slice stems and add to boiling water, simmer 3 minutes. Add leaves and grate ginger over the top of all. Simmer 5 minutes. Kale should be bright green and tender when done.

BAKED OR STEAMED APPLES
Core 4 apples. In bowl place 4 pats butter, 2 tsp. raw honey, 1 tsp. cinnamon, and 1 T sesame seeds. Mix and place in apples. Place apple on steamer rack in pot with water or in pan for oven. Bake for about 1 hr at 350˙.

SPROUTED GRAINS OR LEGUMES
Sprouting grains or legumes releases nutrients and reduces the need to cook them. They can be used in salads, frittatas, or as toppings in sandwiches (substitute spelt bread for wheat bread). To sprout, place in bowl and cover the grain or legume with water and let stand out of refrigerator 20 minutes. Drain the water very well, cover the bowl with a damp cloth. Rinse with tepid water, drain, rinse cloth and wring out, and cover bowl each day until they sprout.

FRESH-FRUIT DRINKS
 (fresh or frozen)Using blender
1 ripe banana
1/2 cup peach
1 cup peach juice

1 ripe banana
1/2 cup blueberries
1 cup apple juice

1 ripe peach
1/2 cup blueberries
1 cup apple juice

WILD RICE WITH HERBS

1 1/2 cups wild rice, washed and drained
1 cup onion, minced
2 cloves garlic, minced
1/2 Tbsp. fresh parsley, minced
1/2 Tbsp. fresh sage, minced
1/2 Tbsp. fresh thyme, chopped fine
1/2 tsp. fresh ground pepper
1 tsp. salt
6 Tbsp. olive oil
4 1/2 cups water

In large saucepan sauté herbs and salt and pepper in oil until aromatic. Add rice and sauté 3-4 minutes. Add onion and garlic and sauté until tender add 2 Tbsp. more oil if needed. Add water, bring to boil, lower heat to simmer, cover and cook 35 minutes or until done. Uncover and heat over low heat shaking the pan until rice is dry and fluffy.

AVOCADO SPREAD

2 medium ripe avocados
salt
1 tsp. cumin
1/4 cup finely minced onion
1 garlic clove, finely minced
2 Tbsp. lemon juice

Mash avocados and mix spices, onion, garlic and lemon juice into the mashed avocados. Serve on bread or crackers.

BARBECUE SAUCE

1/3 cup olive oil
3 Tbsp. lime juice
1 tsp. chopped parsley
1/2 tsp. oregano
1/2 tsp. ground cumin
1/2 tsp. cilantro
1/4 tsp. chili powder; black pepper to taste

Blend in bowl. Let stand 10 minutes.
Baste meat or vegetable burgers while baking or barbecuing

FRITTATA WITH HERBS AND ONIONS

1 cup parsley, chopped fine
2 green onions, trimmed and sliced
1/2 leek, washed and white and pale green parts chopped fine
1/4 cup spinach leaves chopped(stems removed)
1/8 cup chopped mint leaves
2 Tbsp. olive oil for cooking vegetables
1/4 tsp. black pepper
8 eggs, beaten
2 Tbsp. butter
2 Tbsp. olive oil
salt to taste.

Sauté parsley, green onions, leek spinach and mint leaves in two Tbsp. olive oil. Measure no more than 1/2 cup vegetable mixture for every two eggs. Mix eggs with all vegetables and herbs in medium size bowl. Mix butter and oil in small bowl. Pour half the butter mixture into heated skillet, pour half the egg mixture, lower heat, cover and cook approximately 7 minutes until done but not dry. Repeat with second half of mixture.

MUSHROOM VEGETABLE STOCK

In 6 quart pot, place 1 large onion, 2 leeks, 2 stalks celery, 2 carrots, 1 head garlic with skins and cut in half, 1 cup dried mushrooms, 2 stalks parsley, 1/2 tsp. thyme, 1 bay leaf, 1/2 tsp. freshly ground pepper, 2 tsp. salt. Add 12 cups water, simmer 2 hours, adding water if vegetables are not covered. Strain and press vegetables to extract as much broth as possible. Cool and refrigerate or freeze. Should make 5 cups. Use this as a base for miso broth. Simply add miso to taste. Add thin slices of *nori* sea vegetable and fresh chopped parsley, scallion and/or ginger. Kids love it!

Chapter 7

The Importance of Detoxifying

Detoxification. What is it? Why is it important? Is it necessary?

It is not as scary as it sounds, and it is necessary because it strengthens your immune system, enhances your digestion, and allows your body to rejuvenate.

Detoxification is the process of removing toxins from your body. Toxins are harmful substances or organisms that interfere with optimum health. Parasites, bacteria, heavy metals, chemical residues, and excess hormones present in commercial meat and poultry are a few examples. They accumulate primarily in the liver and intestinal tract, but may be found anywhere in the body. Toxins weaken the immune system, and inhibit the body's ability to combat illness.

To detoxify is to cleanse. The purpose is to give your insides a "fresh start" by reducing the toxic burden the body is carrying. Think of it as spring cleaning. Basically there are dozens of ways to cleanse. Some are gentle. Others are not. We do not recommend colonics or enemas for young children. Children are resilient. They will respond very quickly to the most gentle methods of cleansing. The addition of psyllium husk powder to the diet (for a limited time) is gentle. Psyllium husk powder increases fiber and aids elimination. Vegetable juices, prepared from foods they are not allergic to, are good detoxifiers for children. Cat's claw tea, milk thistle seed extract or capsules, garlic capsules, and parsley are all excellent for children. See the resource directory in the back of this book for information on how to obtain some of the above mentioned items.

Adults have a few more options. Most adults can fast for five days drinking only spring water or purified well water that is free of chloride, fluoride, manufacturing waste and agricultural chemicals. There are exceptions. Refer to *Dr. Marshall Mandell's 5-Day Allergy Relief System* for complete instructions. Fasting is one type of cleanse. There are others. Some are rather extensive. A detailed program of cleansing that does not involve fasting can be found in *Cleanse and Purify Thyself* by Richard Anderson, N.D. Again, these intensive cleanses are not for everyone. A persons age and condition must be considered. A fast should not be attempted without a physical examination and approval of your personal physician.

During a fast, the body is free of all food exposures. The body eliminates waste at this time. Headaches, fatigue, joint and muscle pains, "colds," diarrhea, and other chronic symptoms may occur as a result of this. Don't worry about these things. Instead, welcome them. The body is doing its job. Other reactions, such as addictive allergic withdrawal often occurs. These symptoms may range from mild fatigue to severe rage. If symptoms are severe or unusual, consult with your doctor.

Herbal Cleanses.

Sarsaparilla, dandelion, and Oregon grape root are effective herbs for cleansing the blood and stimulating liver detoxification. Other cleansing herbs are stinging nettles, red clover, hawthorn, alfalfa, sage, and burdock root. An herbal detox tea may include birch leaves, parsley leaves, verbena leaves or cat's claw. (among others)

Herbal cleanses may be used in conjunction with a juice fast if you wish. There are herbal detox kits available that will guide you through the cleanse step by step. An herbal cleanse is best combined with or followed by a colon cleanse.

Cleanse the Colon, Too

In the early 1900's, Dr. J.H. Tilden of Denver, Colorado specialized in healing pneumonia, which was then the number one killer. He had more pneumonia cases than any other doctor and he claimed that he never lost a patient. He used no drugs at all. He simply cleaned out the colon, used water therapy, and administered natural, live foods. Even in those days his success was considered phenomenal because other doctors were relying on drugs and antiserums and continually meeting with failure. It has been said that most degenerative diseases are attributable in some way, directly or indirectly, to an unhealthy digestive tract.

As Dr. Bernard Jensen puts it: " . . . When the bowel is dirty, the blood is dirty, and so on to the organs and tissues . . . it is the bowel that invariably has to be cared for first before any effective healing can take place."

And pediatrician, Esteban Genao, M.D. adds, "Cleansing our bowels through enzymes, friendly bacteria, herbs, and the use of proper diet will help rid parasites to decrease toxicity successfully, and this will lead to having a healthy intestinal tract."

It is beneficial to add vegetable juices to your diet or in place of some meals. You can either purchase vegetable juices in the health food store (organic), or juice your own if you happen to own a juicer-extractor. Blender's won't do. Carrot and beets mixed with greens and celery actually taste good to most people. Three or four days of this once a month is healthy for your digestive system and will begin the detoxifying process.

There's so much to learn!

Water Detoxifies Us Daily

A very important part of detoxifying on a daily basis is drinking plenty of pure water. Our bodies are made up mostly of water and to remain healthy we need to drink lots of water every day to replace losses and eliminate wastes. Unfortunately, we have to find a reliable source of pure water or prepare our own.

Municipal water is generally chlorinated and fluoridated making it unsafe to drink for many individuals. In commercial farming areas pesticides and other agrochemical contaminants have leeched underground and entered the water supply. Toxic waste disposal sites may present a problem in your area. Therefore it is very important to think about the source of your water and what type of water processing system will best suit your needs in the years to come.

Water treatment systems with filtration devices can remove some harmful substances. Reverse-osmosis and distillers take out some of the contaminants, but also remove most of the minerals. Many bottled water companies use these types of filtration units, therefore you must add mineral supplements back to the water or face compromises in your health. Most filters do not remove harmful bacteria, parasites, Giardia, or other pathogens unless they are equipped with sub-micron ceramic filters or ultra-violet lights. New technology combines many filters to provide maximum protection. Units that remove chlorine, pesticides, heavy metals such as lead and aluminum, asbestos, nitrates, chemical gases, harmful coliform bacteria and parasites, are preferred.

In any case, with any water purification treatment system it is best to **add back, in a useable form, the minerals removed, as processing creates mostly dead water, devoid of life sustenance**. Minerals can be easily added back in the form of liquid electrolyte crystalloid trace minerals.

Detoxification is an ongoing process. As long as we live, our bodies are excreting waste materials or *detoxifying*. We excrete wastes through the bowel, the kidneys, and through perspiration. Unfortunately, there is often more waste entering the body then can be efficiently eliminated on a daily basis. That it why it is important to *detoxify* the body from time to time using a more intensive method of cleansing. Some people cleanse once a month. Others cleanse once a year. The choice is an individual one and depends upon one's condition and one's objectives for health and well being.

An approach complementary to other types of detoxification and bowel cleansing programs is *cellular detoxification*. Allen M. Kratz, PharmD, has developed a specific program for ADD and ADHD that considers cellular toxicity as a predisposing or contributing factor in these disorders. This program is based on increasing the body's vitality to eliminate cellular toxins and is known as the homeovitic approach. Practitioners using homeovitics will begin with a clearing of all eliminative organs/systems and will follow with specific detox regimens for chemicals, heavy metals and viruses, the three deepest and most problematic toxicities. During both clearing and cellular detox, a homeovitic support formulation is employed to minimize any release responses. In most ADD/ADHD cases, this clearing and detox protocol lasts 48 days. Some practitioners recommend using homeovitics on a preventive basis, once weekly, after the initial cellular detox.

Dr Gregory Ellis, a Certified Nutrition Specialist, uses the homeovitic approach to :"clean and strengthen the foundation before rebuilding with nutrition." Dr. Ellis has had success even in treating autism. He credits cellular detoxification for much of this success and feels it also plays a vital role in overcoming ADD/ADHD.

Chapter 8

Supplements That We Need

What supplements do we *need*? We should take only what we need. Most people need trace minerals, digestive enzymes, and essential fatty acids. Beyond these it is an individual road.

Taking individual vitamins or minerals—magnesium, zinc, or vitamin B6 for example—may be necessary for certain individuals who exhibit symptoms of deficiencies. But, to avoid creating an imbalance in your body chemistry through the indiscriminate use of supplements, it would be prudent consult a natural health care practitioner. Amino acid supplementation may be called for, but again, it is difficult for us to say which ones YOU should take.

For now, let's look at the basics. The fundamental nutrients that everyone needs and which many people lack are: trace minerals, enzymes, and essential fatty acids.

Trace Minerals

At least eleven trace minerals have been recognized as essential for human development and over all health. These are copper, iron, zinc, cobalt, iodine, molybdenum, manganese, magnesium, selenium, chromium, and fluorine.

Trace mineral deficiencies can cause anxiety, limited attention span, and short term memory problems. Severe depression, which strikes one in fifty American teens, has been linked to deficiencies of copper, molybdenum, vanadium, and zinc. A person lacking dietary copper and chromium may have difficulty with their blood sugar levels at the cellular level. Abnormal blood sugar fluctuations can produce violent behavior, mood swings, fatigue, and irritability. An adequate supply of minerals, properly balanced, is necessary for health.

Trace mineral deficits in the body do not always stem from dietary deficiencies. Diets high in simple sugars, sucrose and fructose, reduce the body's ability to *use and retain* copper and chromium—two of the very minerals necessary for regulating blood sugar.

Low iron levels may impair judgment, reasoning ability, and all aspects of left brain activity, including scientific, math, and spoken and written language skills. Anemia has conventionally been treated by giving iron supplements. It has been found that, in some cases, anemia may be attributable to a vitamin C deficiency. Vitamin C boosts iron absorption and must be present for iron to be assimilated.

In chapter three we talked about the importance of amino acids. (see pp. 15-17). Amino acids are very important, BUT, to work properly, amino acids require the presence of the correct balance of *minerals.* Minerals are the building blocks...the basics, and when they are combined in a solution of water, trace minerals create electrolytes, the spark of life.

The ideal solution is to take a mineral supplement that has all the needed trace minerals in the proper combination. Minerals come in different forms. *Crystalloid* minerals are in a form so small that they can easily permeate the cell wall. The next largest form of well absorbed minerals (from salt beds for example,) are *ionic* in form. *Chelated* minerals from plants (grown in mineral rich soil, free from agrochemicals, pesticides, and insecticides) are larger yet, but again can be used readily by the body. *Colloidal* mineral supplements, because of their larger size, have been found to be more difficult for the body to absorb. Parts of this form of mineral that can't get through the cell wall, remain in the bloodstream and may be deposited in the vascular system causing problems such as kidney stones.

Enzymes

It has been well documented through animal studies, especially those conducted by Dr. Francis Pottenger in the 1930's, that a cooked food diet depletes the body's natural enzymes, resulting in old age diseases showing up long before old age. We are seeing this trend in our young people—short term memory loss, ailments of the colon and digestive tract, pancreatitus, arthritis, ulcers—not what you might expect of one of the wealthiest countries in the world. Or is it?

Enzymes are essential in maintaining internal cleanliness, health, youth, and strength. Dr. Richard Anderson considers them to be, "Far more important than any other nutrient." He says, "Proteins cannot be utilized without enzymes, nor can vitamins and minerals. Enzymes are destroyed after use and must be constantly replaced. Cooked foods draw from the enzyme reserves, depleting the body's precious 'labor force.'"

According to Dr. Edward Howell, who, Anderson says, "Is probably the world's authority on enzymes," *each person is given a limited supply of body enzyme at birth.* Howell believes that many, if not all, degenerative diseases from which humans suffer and die are caused by excessive use of enzyme deficient cooked and processed foods. Read *Enzyme Nutrition* by Dr. Edward Howell.

Enzymes are produced by the pancreas. When cooked and processed foods use up enzymes at every meal, the pancreas gets tired. This compromises the immune system and may complicate the symptoms of ADD/ADHD. Raw foods contain their own enzymes, but when we cook the food we kill the enzymes. Therefore the food is not digested unless the pancreas supplies the digestive enzymes. Undigested food in the intestinal tract provides food for bacteria and parasites. In addition, if digestion is not functioning properly, then protein can't be broken down into free form amino acids, which then are unable to produce serotonin for the proper functioning of the brain.(see pp. 16-18).

To reduce the extra work of the pancreas and to conserve your supply of body enzymes, you can supplement your diet with plant enzymes every time you eat cooked or processed food. This type of enzyme works throughout the digestive tract, whereas some types just work in the stomach. Benefits include less stomach and intestinal diseases as well as prevention of arthritis which some have referred to as an enzyme deficiency disease.

Essential Fatty Acids

From all the emphasis on low fat diets and fat free foods, one would think that fat is a body's worst enemy, but that really isn't the case. Some often overlooked fats that are *essential* to life are the Omega 3 and Omega 6 fats, known as *essential fatty acids,* or EFA'S. These can not be made by the body, and therefore, must be ingested as food. Many people are deficient in these essential fats because their diets lack the foods that contain these nutrients.

EFA's aid transmission of nerve impulses that are needed for normal brain functioning—this is their direct connection to treating people with ADD/ADHD. The brain is about 60 percent fat, and just as the body is 75 percent water and requires a daily supply of water to survive, the brain requires essential fatty acids.

EFA's are food for the brain.

EFA's also support cardiovascular health and energy metabolism, and they help a person handle stress. They are helpful in most skin conditions, visual function, fertility, and many other complex functions of the body. Obvious indications of EFA imbalance are brittle nails, dry skin, hair loss, depression, ringing of the ears, cold intolerance, chronic pain, irritable bowel syndrome, asthma, arthritis and migraines.

We all need essential fatty acid supplementation, but in the case of those with ADD/ADHD it is not only recommended, it is *essential*.

Unfortunately, these essential oils are easily damaged by **heat, light and oxygen**. Commercially made oils are a very poor source of EFA's. This results from the oil being heated during pressing, and being stored for long periods of time on the shelf.

Essential fatty acids can be obtained from supplemental sources. The best sources of these UNPROCESSED oils are: Organic flax seed meal, cold pressed flax seed oil, borage oil, salmon oil, evening primrose oil, and black currant oil. Oils are available in liquid and capsule form. Fish, especially cod and salmon, are the most common food sources of essential fatty acids. Cod liver oil is readily available as a supplement. Flax seed as a supplement, is something that can be used every day and it tastes delicious! Ground flax seed can be used in cooking. It can also be sprinkled on cereal, which is a great way to deliver EFA's to children.

Traditionally, oils were pressed slowly and without heat. Then they were sold and used within a week or so as they were considered a perishable food item. Processing that uses high pressure and heat, destroys the oils beneficial qualities. Processing increases the shelf life, making storage and distribution more convenient for the manufacturers. A long shelf life, however, means that the oil is no longer a "live" food. You can prove this by leaving margarine out of the refrigerator and seeing how long it takes for it to spoil, or even for anything to grow in it. It will likely be years if at all.

Avoid all hydrogenated or partially hydrogenated oils. The intake of these types of oils may contribute to clogged arteries, weight gain, fatigue, lowered immunity, and poor mental function.

Read labels and stay away from foods containing these treated oils (margarine, commercial cooking oil, most commercial snack and prepared foods). Butter is better and if you want to use oil, use cold pressed virgin olive oil. Make sure the oil comes in a light proof bottle because light destroys the beneficial qualities of the oil. If you are using flax seed, make sure it is fresh. A bitter taste may indicate rancidity.

Rhodiola rosea herb
This adaptogenic herb, used for centuries in Russia, has reportedly influenced learning and focusing in ADD patients. Studies have revealed that the process of learning and focusing is supported by interactions between various chemical transmitters in the brain. Among these are norepinephrine (noradrenaline) which can improve learning and focusing when its levels are modulated. The active ingredient, salidroside, in Rodiola rosea (Rosavin™), has the ability to regulate norepinephrine and dopamine. In one study, therapeutic effects were obtained with ADD patients exhibiting mental and physical fatigue, lack of concentration and hyperactivity. The study showed a decrease in symptoms within three weeks, with the results being so successful that dosage was cut in half.

The success of the herb depends upon the harvesting time (spring) as the effectiveness of its constituents are at maximum potency early in the growing season. If you purchase supplements, please inquire as to the time of harvest, for your protection.

Chapter 9

Nutrients that Help ADD/ADHD

Amino acids. DMG (Dimethylglycine): Technically classified as a food and resembling water soluble vitamins such as the B vitamins, DMG is found in small amounts in foods such as rice hulls. After its discovery, DMG was initially used to help autistic children. It has been shown to improve behavior, reduce frustration, and improve speech. GABA (gamma-aminobutric acid): Useful in treating anxiety in children and adults. Acts as a safe and mild tranquilizer. Prolonged stress, panic, or fear, may indicate the need for GABA supplementation. Glutamine: A conditionally essential amino acid used to make neurotransmitters which help you feel calm and focused, while reducing sugar cravings and hypoglycemic reactions. Phenylalanine: an essential amino acid that is necessary for neurotransmitter production. Phenylalanine as a natural food supplement should not be confused with the chemically altered form used in aspartame. Taurine: A non essential amino acid. It has been known to help control hyperactivity and reduce excessive movement. Tyrosine: A semi-essential amino acid that converts to the amino acid, L-Dopa. Has been administered for depression and hypertension.

Bee Pollen. This is the bee's vitamin pill as it contains vitamins, minerals, enzymes, amino acids, lecithin and fructose. It is used to treat anemia, obesity, diarrhea, skin problems and mental illness.

Calcium/Magnesium. Calcium and magnesium work in unison. It is usually not a good idea to take one without the other as this can cause an imbalance. If there is already an imbalance—which is often the case with people who have ADD/ADHD—then this may indicate the need for taking one or the other for a *limited time*. It may be helpful to have a tissue analysis test done first. (see resource directory). Too much calcium can deplete the body of magnesium. Depleted magnesium levels are almost always found in people with ADD/ADHD. Other symptoms of magnesium deficiency may include, apprehensiveness, irritability, confusion, noise sensitivity, muscle spasms, back and neck pain, anxiety, and fatigue. Too little calcium may cause sleep disturbances, anger, and inattentiveness.

Cat's Claw. This herb, Una de Gato, works as an anti-inflammatory and as an immune system activator. Amazing results have occurred within 48 hours after beginning use of this herb when treating ear infections and depression. Cat's Claw at the cellular level, is quick and effective. It helps to regulate our body's pH balance, thereby enhancing the digestive capabilities which in turn, facilitates the absorption of nutrients. An ill functioning digestive system will be the base for many of our maladies, including brain disorder. Esteban A. Genao, M.D., pediatrician, states, "In ADD or ADHD, it is clear that there are imbalances of some neurotransmitters (our message delivery system). These neurotransmitters are formed by amino acids, which come from our digestion of protein. If the pH in the stomach is high, digestion of protein will be incomplete, thereby compromising neurotransmitter formation. This can affect the brain and may manifest as a behavioral anomaly or learning disability. Cat's Claw can improve the digestion and assimilation of nutrients, thereby supporting the immune system and reducing the effects of maldigestion related behavioral disorders."

Garlic. As garlic proponents know, this popular food has been a natural remedy for centuries. It's been called the miracle cure, used for colds, sore throats, as protection from virus, bacteria, parasites, and fungus, and topically, to ward off wound infections. Much research into the benefits of aged garlic extract (AGE) has been done and we now know how truly beneficial this little clove is. AGE offers liver protection, prevents cancer, reduces blood clot formation (when it's not needed for wound healing), inhibits candida albicans (the bad intestinal yeast) and helps strengthen the good colon flora. It keeps blood from sticking to arterial walls thus preventing blood clots, and acts as an effective free-radical fighter. In addition to the numerous benefits of AGE, people with ADD or ADHD should consider adding this supplement, as it has been reported to enhance brain nutrition and improve memory. It is very helpful for stress reduction by lowering corticoid, a hormone secreted by the body during stress and it can fight ear infections, which are common in many allergic young children who are later diagnosed with ADD.

Green Foods. Dark green leafy vegetables, chlorophyll, blue green algae, kelp, spirulina, kamut, wheat grass, and barley grass and other supplements can provide us with the tools to fortify the immune system. Used in conjunction with magnesium, calcium, and other trace minerals, green supplements support the body's basic nutritional needs.

Chlorella helps rid the body of free radicals. This increases the efficiency of your immune system to protect you from bacteria, viruses and cancer cells. Chlorophyll, called "concentrated sun power" is very effective against bacteria and can actually be more effective than vitamin A, C or E as an antioxidant. It also helps to alkalize blood pH.

Sea vegetables such as kelp, spirulina, and blue green algae, provide a high source of micronutrients. Kelp sparks vital enzyme reactions in the body and supports the thyroid. Hawaiian Spirulina is considered one of the premium green superfoods. It is a concentrated whole food source of phyto-nutrients, supplying a rich mixture of carotenoids, chlorophyll, enzymes, complete vegetarian protein, B-vitamins, and a newly discovered anti-viral compound called calcium spirulan. Blue green algae is nutrient dense. Small doses can provide biologically active vitamins, minerals, trace elements, amino acids, simple carbohydrates, enzymes, fatty acids, carotenoids and chlorophyll. It's protein content is of a type that may be more easily broken down and assimilated by the body than the proteins in meat and vegetables.

Dehydrated cereal grasses such as wheat and barley, are extremely high in protein. Dehydrated cereal grasses contain 25 percent protein whereas milk contains 3 percent, eggs 12 percent and steak 16 percent. This information is valuable when one is considering protein alternatives to animal products. Cereal grass contains all the essential amino acids and therefore is a good alternative to meat, milk or eggs.

Lecithin. This fat like substance is normally produced in the liver. Nutrients enter and leave your cells via cell membranes mostly composed of lecithin. If its in short supply, this membrane will harden and nutrients will be kept out. The best thing lecithin does is to dissolve the bad cholesterol in the blood. It can also help with memory loss, and assist with absorption of fat soluble vitamins because it is an emulsifier (makes two unlike substances able to merge).

Nutritional (not Brewer's) Yeast. This nutrient is a concentrated source of your B vitamins and minerals (iron, potassium, calcium, chromium) and is a high quality protein with very little fat. Nutritional yeast that is slow extracted, and high protein yielding (about 70%,) can be extremely beneficial in restoring balance in the body. This form of protein is high in RNA. The supplementation of a product of this nature can greatly enhance brain function.

Proanthocyanidins. Proanthocyanidins are powerful antioxidants with the ability to cross the blood-brain barrier. They promote clearer thinking. This substance is most commonly found in dark-colored grape seeds and pine bark. Parents have reported success with hyperactive children using these supplements alone. In laboratory studies, dark colored grape seed extract as well pine bark were shown to be more powerful antioxidants than vitamins, E, C, beta-carotene and even a combination of E and C. Some grape seed supplements may contain pesticides, or are processed with toxins. Reliable companies use organically grown grapes and clean extraction methods. Therefore, to be sure you're getting a true natural product, read labels or contact the manufacturer and ask questions before you purchase.

Zinc. Zinc controls protein synthesis in every cell of the body. Zinc is important in wound healing, can reduce inflammation, tone down body odor, boost the immune system, prevent toxic effects of heavy metals like cadmium, and improve brain function. Children who are hyperactive or aggressive from high copper levels, can benefit from zinc supplements which will reduce the copper levels. Beware of playing master chemist, as overdoses can lead to fever, nausea, vomiting, diarrhea, and cause iron and normal levels of copper to leach from the body contributing to anemia. Zinc deficiency has been linked to ADD and other behavioral problems. Esteban Genoa, M.D., pediatrician, effectively treats ADD children with zinc and trace minerals, along with making certain changes in the diet.

Flower Essences. Flower essences are a old form of nutrient/vibrational medicine redeveloped back in the early 1930's. As some of you reading this may already know, they work by reaching into the deeper emotional sections of our minds and our bodies, where they directly affect change. In this way, flower essences are often explained as being an emotional medicine, targeting the underlying emotions that effect us from day to day. Following this train of thought, it is simple to realize that if emotions have such a great effect on our mental outlook, they must also have a huge effect on us physically.

These flower remedies, as they are sometimes called, have been used for anything from medical emergencies, like car accidents, to extreme grief resulting from the death of a loved one. In this way, they have bridged a gap that exists in our current Western medical theories. Flower remedies address a type of medicine for the body that we normally answer by the use of very strong drugs. Self-doubt is a common emotion found in people labeled ADD. This type of emotional "illness," difficult to treat with synthetic drugs, may be helped by using flower remedies. What's more, these medicines are normally considered safe enough to be used with any other medications.

There are several flower essences that have had positive results in treating ADD and ADHD. One product helps flighty children to become centered and more focused, by grounding their thoughts and helping to control the distractions that come from seemingly everywhere. There are flower remedies for stress and tension which work both for parents and also for ADHD children who always have to be doing something. This remedy eases the pressures that many ADD/ADHD children have from school, parents, friends, aloneness, or the expectations created by media input. Flower remedies can also assist children who forget or "zone out." When we look at treating the symptoms of ADD/ADHD, we must not forget the emotional side and the help that may come from flowers.

Peruvian herbs. A Peruvian herb, royal maca has been shown to improve the ability to focus and create a calming effect, along with improving one's ability to sleep sound. It is a nutritional powerhouse that is especially rich iodine, amino acids, complex carbohydrates and ease minerals such as iron, zinc, phosphorus, calcium magnesium. Maca also contains various vitamins such B₂, B₁₂, C and E. Testimonials from parents of child ADD have shown improvement in concentration wh in water, ½ tsp. daily of maca and another Per çamu camu.

Chapter 10

Non-Dietary Approaches to ADD/ADHD

Hair Mineral Analysis. As discussed in the section on minerals, imbalances can contribute to behavioral and learning disabilities. One method used to discover your imbalance, is through hair analysis. Labs report a breakdown of your *intracellular* (not blood) mineral levels along with symptoms you may experience, from deficiencies or excess of calcium, magnesium, boron, selenium, copper, potassium, sodium, etc. Toxic levels of heavy metals that can contribute to symptoms of ADD/ADHD can also be tested in this manner. (Hair analysis is used by the Environmental Protection Agency to detect the presence of toxic metals in the body). In order to assure consistency in diagnosis, it is extremely important to choose a *government approved* laboratory for this type of analysis. Based on these laboratory reports, if you chose to follow a mineral rebalancing program, you should be retested in three months to determine your progress. Adding a comprehensive mineral supplement to the diet should always be preferred to taking individual minerals. Please consult with a practitioner prior to entertaining a supplement program, and request a mineral analysis in order to ascertain how to properly balance your body.

Phase Contrast Microscopy Analysis. Useful as a diagnostic tool, this live blood analysis may indicate toxic elements in the blood, such as yeast, bacteria and parasites. Through this analysis, the practitioner can determine both acute and chronic conditions affecting one's health. Compromised immune systems have been discovered in a number of children with ADD/ADHD/Autism, who have had their blood tested through Phase Contrast Microscopy analysis. These analysis' have revealed yeasts, parasites, heavy metal intoxication, liver stress, adrenal stress, bacteria, fat digestion difficulties, allergies, pH imbalances and other anomalies. High levels of toxicity in the blood may indicate inadequate levels of oxygen and an overtaxed immune system. Immune system breakdown has been linked to varying levels of brain dysfunction. For a practitioner nearest you, contact the American Institute for Medical and Nutritional Microscopy (941)-966-7337.

Atlas Subluxation Adjustment. A specific chiropractic adjustment may be all that is needed to relieve symptoms of ADD in certain people. Carlo Longobardo, D.C., C.A.O. (Certified Atlas Orthogonist), explains, "For some time now, there seems to be an agreement and growing concern that the brain stem is under an abnormal pressure in patients with ADD."

"David was diagnosed with A.D.D. after tests showed he had "deep rooted angers and fears." He was put on Ritalin and requested that the school consider psychotherapy as an alternative to the drug. They refused. David's mother changed schools. He then began upper cervical chiropractic treatment and after 3 1/2 weeks, his parent began taking him off the Ritalin. Since that time he has been tested as "normal" and only has problems in music class because he is still sensitive to noise. He takes pride in the fact that he can control himself by himself, and as a result is working harder in school. In three years of testing, frustration and anxiety, his parents were never told that atlas chiropractic therapy was a possible alternative."
—Dr. Michael Halliday, D.C.

Misalignment of the top vertebra in the neck (called the Atlas) creates a condition known as the Atlas Subluxation Complex, meaning, simply, that the Atlas is out of place. This causes direct pressure on the brain stem and

70

prohibits the travel of proper neural signals from the brain to the lower body.

People with ADD/ADHD who have difficulty controlling the movement of their limbs may be experiencing this restriction. A signal for movement gets short circuited on its way through the brain stem preventing the arm from reacting as desired. Atlas Orthogony is a simple procedure, done on an Atlas machine in a chiropractor's office, that may correct the problem and provide relief from the symptoms of ADD/ADHD. For the name of a practitioner nearest you, call (770)-457-4430.

Craniosacral Therapy. Craniosacral therapy works by gently adjusting the craniosacral system (the brain and spinal cord) with pressures equal to that of the weight of a nickel on the palm of one's hand. Dr. John Upledger, D.O., O.M.M., founder of the Upledger Institute in Palm Beach Gardens, FL insists that some cases of ADD could be considered as a symptom of an underlying misalignment or malfunction of some kind. His research and experience with children displaying hyperactive behavior led him to determine that not only could emotional problems, and food and chemical intolerance contribute to ADD/ADHD behavior, but a dysfunction in the craniosacral system could be a key factor also. Many times the birth process or an accident at a young age can change the position of the head on the neck. Through procedures Dr. Upledger developed in releasing blockages in the neck, and skull (areas surrounding the brain stem and occipital bone), he discovered hyperactive children calmed down, sometimes immediately. This beneficial therapy is non-invasive, non-drug and can assist in helping behavioral problems *and* improve over all health and well being.

Aromatherapy. Aromatherapy uses the aromatic essence of plant extracts. Lavender, Orange, and peppermint are most useful in cases of ADD or ADHD. Lavender balances the central nervous system and is used as a sleep aid and to help hyperactive children feel calm. Orange is used to encourage relaxation. Peppermint supports mental activities and stabilizes the emotions. Essential oils can be dispensed in a diffuser, a mister or by inhalation by placing drops on a cloth or your skin. Warning: Do not wear citrus oils on your skin out in the sun, discoloration may result.

Flower Remedies. Homeopathic preparations of flowering plants and trees have been known to alleviate many emotional and psychological problems. In cases of ADD, feelings of discouragement, failure, insecurity, lethargy, and frustration may be lessened with the help of flower remedies. People with a lack of concentration may be helped by Clematis; discouragement lessened by Gentian; motivation may be bolstered through Wild Rose; and stress lessened with a common five flower remedy. These preparations are commonly administered by sublingual application (under the tongue) and can be found in most health food stores.

Homeopathic Remedies. These preparations are dilution's (to an infinitesimal degree) of natural plant, mineral, and animal substances. They work on the principle "like cures like." As an example, a treatment for a skin problem, may be made from the poison ivy plant. Delivered in micro-doses, they are safe for children, pregnant women and the elderly and they can be used alone or in combination with conventional treatment. Homeopathics may be of help with symptoms related to ADD. A good homeopathic doctor will be able to choose the correct remedy for you or your child. Homeopathic preparations should be stored in a light-proof container, away from electrical appliances which may tend to weaken the potency.

Herbs. Could be considered a dietary measure. Nature has provided us with medicinal plants. Herbs used for symptoms of ADD/ADHD include catnip, valerian root, lemon balm, licorice root, chamomile and rosemary. Calming effects can be seen through the use of mullein and lobelia, which are antispasmodics. Scullcap and valerian root, chamomile, passion flower, lemon balm and catnip are also used to calm nerves and muscles, and to promote regular and restful sleep. Herbs that can increase blood flow and oxygen circulation to the head, improving memory, nerve response and mental alertness are St. John's wort, gotu kola, and ginkgo biloba. Herbs that regulate blood sugar are beet root, licorice, catnip, lemon grass, hibiscus, peppermint, and nettles. Gingko biloba is also effective in treating inner ear balance problems.

Tachyonized energy. *Tachyon energy*, otherwise known as "life force" energy has been proven to have an integral part in the healing realm. When life force energy is blocked, our electrical system can short circuit preventing our body from reacting properly to neural impulses. There are now scientific methods of restructuring certain materials at the sub-molecular level, that then become antennae to attract and focus usable biological energy, *Tachyon energy*. Tachyon beads when placed on specific areas of the body, can provide remarkable healing results. Tests have shown that when these beads are placed on the head, they magnify the flow of energy to the brain and therefore may be useful in treating ADD/ADHD.

A mother from Austin Texas tells us that her 18 year old son had been diagnosed with ADHD 12 years ago. He tried medications, herbs, homeopathy and dietary "remedies." Most recently he started wearing a headband with a Tachyon cell affixed to it on the left side of his head. This had the effect of calming him down. He also relaxes twice a week in a Tachyon Cocoon which seems to help him with his focus and balance.

Educational Kinesiology. Developmental specialists have been using movements that enhance learning for over 50 years. Paul Dennison, Ph.D., the creator of Educational Kinesiology, took these movements into his learning disabilities clinics and simplified them, discovered why the movements hadn't worked for some people, and developed techniques that make them effective for everyone. The new movements are called Brain Gym® movements. Normal brain function requires efficient communication between the many nuclei or functional centers located throughout the brain. Learning and functional disabilities occur when information cannot flow freely between these centers of the brain. The Brain Gym movements stimulate this flow of information within the brain, restoring our innate ability to learn and function at top efficiency. For information contact the Educational Kinesiology Foundation at (805) 658-7942.

Brainwave Synchronizing. Special patterns of sound frequencies have been scientifically demonstrated to synchronize brainwave activity in the two hemispheres. Hemispheric synchronization has great value for people with ADD and ADHD. Remarkable improvements in ability to focus, longer attention span and calmer emotions have occurred from listening to audiotapes and CDs that contain a patented audio technology called Hemi-Sync®. Educators and parents observe that Hemi-Sync seems to improve neurological capacity to integrate information and filter unwanted sensory input. Improved behavior at home and improved school performance demonstrate that youngsters eventually become able to access beneficial brainwave states on their own, without the stimulus of Hemi-Sync. Comparable to bicycle training wheels, Hemi-Sync helps the brain learn how to normalize its functioning. Once learned, the aid is no longer required. For more information contact Interstate Industries, Inc. at (804) 263-8692.

Resource Directory

The statements in this resource directory may not have been evaluated by the Food and Drug Administration. As such, these products may not be intended to diagnose, treat, cure or prevent any disease.

HIDDEN HEALTH MENACES USUALLY OVERLOOKED. Do you know that pinworms are a frequent cause of ADD/ADHD, overlooked by health practitioners? PARASITES, TOXICITY and SENSITIVITY to household/ school/workplace chemical cleaning agents, are major contributing factors to both ADD/ADHD. Discover <u>S</u>imple, <u>A</u>ffordable, <u>F</u>ormulas that are <u>E</u>ffective *"Safe Natural Solutions"* for all the above. For 4 FREE audio tapes contact: NATURAL HEALTH CONCEPTS, P.O. Box 1995, Wallingford, CT 06492 (800)-910-0246 or (800)-555-9205 ext. 6039

AMINO ACID SUPPLEMENT FOR KIDS. It has been said that a child's state of health is equivalent to his or her nutritional make up. For many, hyperactive behavior and learning disorders can be addressed by supplying the cells with the proper nutrient mix. *Kids Plex Jr.* is a complete, balanced nutritional supplement, high in amino acids recognized by experts as "the primary building blocks of human life." *Kids Plex Jr.* has 100% of the RDA of vitamins and nutrients needed by a growing child. The powdered form is easy to mix in juice or sprinkled on food. Kids Plex Jr is nutritional insurance for your family's health. A product of NATURADE, available at G.N.C. and other fine health & nutrition stores. For information call (800)-933-7539 NATURADE, INC., P.O. Box 700-474, Dallas TX 75370 website: kidsplex@airmail.net

IMMUNE SYSTEM SUPPORT. This company provides a nutrient rich powdered "green" drink, *Kyo-Green®*, high in amino acids, vitamins and anti-oxidants; *Kyolic®* aged garlic extract to fight heavy metal poisoning, bacteria and infectious disease. They also offer "friendly" strains of intestinal bacteria, *Probiata or Kyodophilus®*, necessary for optimum colon health; as well as *Ginkgo Biloba Plus* for mental health and alertness. WAKUNAGA OF AMERICA, 23501 Madero, Mission Viejo, CA 92692 (800)-825-7888

HAIR MINERAL ANALYSIS IDENTIFIES NUTRITIONAL IMBALANCES. The most accurate way to identify ADD/ADHD is bio-chemically through *Tissue Mineral Analysis*. If not balanced nutritionally, a lifelong usage of medications could be your child's future. A TMA should be performed to avoid all of the pain associated with ADD/ADHD....It's as simple as a Haircut! Provides phone consultation and a graphic presentation of nutritional imbalances. BIO-SPECTRUM ANALYSIS, P.O. Box 572911. Houston, TX 77257 (800)-847-4218

COGNITIVELY CHALLENGED? Pay attention and remember with Ecological Formulas *COGNITIVE NUTRITION*. Contains 300 mg. DMAE Bitartrate, 100 mg. Choline Citrate, 10 mg. Glyclyglutamine, 15 mg. Acetylcarnitine, 10 mg. Niacin, 5 mg. Cytidine Choline, 5 mg. Pyridoxal 5' Phosphate, Thiamine (TTFD), 2 mg. Manganese Picolinate. Ecological Formulas *ESSENTIAL FATTY ACID COMPLEX* is a unique and complete spectrum of EFA's, from Borage, black current seed, safflower, sunflower, sesame and virgin olive oils, lecithin and vitamin E. SEDNA SPECIALTY HEALTH PRODUCTS, P.O. Box 347, Hannibal, MO 63401 (800)-223-0858

DIGESTIVE ENZYMES. *TYME ZYME*™ an *all natural* formula, contains all the necessary enzymes for digestion throughout the intestinal tract. It contains protease, amylase, lipase, cellulase and lactase. When taken with meals, it increases absorption and assures the body of receiving the benefits of vital nutrients, especially zinc, selenium, vitamin B6 and essential fatty acids. Enzymes also guard against maldigestion and associated food allergies, reducing their associated emotional and behavioral effects. PROZYME™ PRODUCTS, LTD. 6600 N. Lincoln Ave., Lincolnwood IL 60645 (800)-522-5537 call Debra Casey for information.

DAKOTA FLAX GOLD. An excellent source of essential fatty acids. All natural edible fresh flax seed, high in lignin's which can be used over cereal, on salads, in soups or in juice. It is low in cadmium and is better tasting that packaged flax products. Available with grinder (seeds must be ground for full nutritional value). Flax, also available in capsule form. S.A.S.E. for sample. HEINTZMAN FARMS, RR2 Box 265, Onaka SD 57466 (800)-333-5813 http://www.heintzmanfarms.com

THE MEDICINE TIN OF ESSENTIAL OILS. THE MEDICINE TIN is a self care kit for the home for making palm blends. It includes Lavender, Tea Tree, Peppermint, Eucalyptus, Orange pure essential oils, organic jojoba base oil, Lavender Mist, Organic cotton flannel cloth and guide book. Audio tapes also available. OIL LADY AROMATHERAPY® 764 12ᵀᴴ Ave., Naples, FL 34102 (941) 263-3451 fax (941) 263-0898

MIGHTY GREENS. This new product is a blend of wheat, barley, rye and oat grass along with spirulina and chlorella. Also included in the formula are 22 other support herbs including ginkgo biloba, ginseng, and grape skin extract. *Mighty Greens* is a super food blend with a strong combination of amino acids, anti-oxidants and other nutrients that support the immune system and all the body functions. PINES INTERNATIONAL, PO Box 1107, Lawrence KS 66044 (800)-697-4637

FLOWER ESSENCES, For A Clearer Mind and Life. A homeopathic-style Deva Flower Remedy®, *Centering/Focus*, effectively clears the mind by easing and calming the emotional/mental issues that cause the chaos within. *Centering/Focus* allows the emotions to subside, aiding the mind with Focus, which may not be there. Also, *Stress/Tension* can be used to reduce the extreme stress misdirected at children of ADD. With the major stimuli blasted throughout our culture, anyone with ADD can benefit from this formula.. NATURAL LABS CORP., PO Box 5351, Lake Montezuma, AZ 86341 (800)-233-0810 Email: Natbio@sedona.net

LIQUID CRYSTALLOID ELECTROLYTE MINERALS. *Trace-Lyte™* is a crystalloid (smallest form) electrolyte formula that helps keep cells strong, balance pH, facilitate removal of toxins and provide the body's life force. If extra magnesium is required, *Cal-Lyte™* offers a 1:1 ratio of calcium/magnesium with boron to assist absorption. Also available is *Total-Lyte™* which increases mental efficiency, improves concentration, nourishes the brain and combats school fatigue.. NATURE'S PATH, INC., PO Box 7862, Venice, FL 34287-7862 (800)-326-5772.

UPLEDGER INSTITUTE. (CRANIOSACRAL THERAPY) Learn more about CranioSacral Therapy and how it can help ease the symptoms of A.D.D. naturally, without medications. Intensive programs for children with A.D.D. and learning disabilities are available. Call for information and/or to order an international directory of practitioners. THE UPLEDGER INSTITUTE HEALTHPLEX CLINICAL SERVICES, 11211 Prosperity Farms Rd., D-223, Palm Beach Gardens, FL 33410-3487 (561) 622-4706

HOMEOPATHIC REMEDIES. Healing begins with cleansing. *The Newton #1 DETOXIFIER* formula stimulates excretion of toxins by the liver and kidneys, spleen & colon. Taken in combination with the *Newton #29 BOWEL DISCOMFORT,* normal digestive and intestinal processes are enhanced (crucial for restoration of children's health). For hyperactivity *SIMILIA #71 HYPERACTIVITY* formula is available through health practitioners. NEWTON, 2360 Rockaway Ind. Blvd., Conyers, GA 30207 (800)-448-7256 FAX (800)-760-5550
E-mail: newtrmdy@avana.net Web: www.newtonlabs.net

HERBS TO CALM AND NOURISH YOUR MIND AND NERVES.
Two herbal formulas, *PreTrac* and *ProTrac* both supply an alternative to drugs for hyperactivity, anxiety and depression. *PreTrac* is used to withdraw safely from prescription medication. *ProTrac* should be used once the drugs are discontinued. Both PreTrac and ProTrac help to clean the blood with detoxifying herbs and Jurassic Green™, a nutrient dense powder from the juice of organic Alfalfa, Barley and Kamut®. Our mission is to remedy the cause of chemical imbalance, not add to the problem.. DR. CHRISTOPHER'S, 1195 Spring Creek Pl, Springville UT 84663 (800)-453-1406

DMG (n,n-Dimethylglycine). DMG is a naturally occurring tertiary amino acid, a product of cellular metabolism. DMG is a nutritive supplement that has been shown to be effective in the treatment of Autism. Improvement has also been reported in ADD/ADHD children. Tradenames: *Food Science Aangamik® DMG* (retail), *DaVinci Gluconic® DMG* (Health Care Professionals). FOODSCIENCE CORP., 20 New England Dr., Essex Junction, VT 05453 (800)-451-5190

CELLULAR DETOXIFICATION AND SUPPORT. Homeovitics for clearing, cellular detoxification and support. A 48 day program is available as a *Protocol Pak* to initiate a natural approach to ADD. The Protocol Pak is used to cleanse the body of cellular toxins, such as chemicals and metals which are a predisposing factor to ADD. Homeovitic formulations are available from your pharmacy or health care professional. For information: HVS LABORATORIES, 3427 Exchange Ave., Naples, FL 34104 (800)-521-7722 web: http://www.hvslabs.com

DIETARY SUPPLEMENT BAR. "Attention"™ is a delicious dietary supplement bar designed to enhance attention span and concentration. This "state of the art" comprehensive formulation, consisting of essential fatty acids, phospholipids, specific vitamins, minerals and botanical compounds, is provided in a unique gluco-regulatory (blood glucose) delivery system without artificial sweeteners. It is great tasting to kids. METABOLIC RESPONSE MODIFIERS, 2633 West Coast Highway, Suite B, Newport Beach, CA 92663 (800)-948-6296 Website: www.metamode.com

ESSENTIAL FATTY ACID (EFA) BALANCER. As necessary ingredients for proper cellular neurotransmitter function in the brain and throughout the body, Omega-3 EFAs must be balanced with Omega-6 EFAs. Flax is the richest source of Omega-3 with a good balance of Omega-6. *Fortified Flax* and *Power Pack Energy Drink* Mix can be sprinkled on cereal and sandwiches or mixed with juice or water. OMEGA-LIFE, INC. PO Box 208, Brookfield, WI 53008-0208 (800)-EAT-FLAX (328-3529)

BALANCED AND COMPLETE MULTI-VITAMIN & MINERAL. *Pro Kids*™ is a uniquely balanced and complete multivitamin and mineral supplement just for kids, with Pycnogenol™ added for optimal antioxidant protection. *Pro Kids*™ chewable tablets are sweetened with dried fruit and natural raspberry flavor. *Maritime Plus*™ antioxidant complex provides a special combination of nutrients that strengthen the body's natural defense mechanism including Gingko Biloba to enhance circulation to the brain for improved memory and concentration. *Enzokaire*™ with Enzogenol™ (pine bark + other OPCs) provides full spectrum antioxidant protection against free radical damage, reduces the effects of stress, increases energy and endurance and may help improve concentration. KAIRE NUTRACEUTICALS, INC. Longmont CO. (800) 870-0036 access code 167   www.kaireint.com

ORGANIC SPROUTED SOY CONCENTRATE & INTESTINAL FLORA PRODUCTS. *REGENEZYME* powder or caplets, is an all natural 100% organic, sprouted whole food concentrate (not a processed or fractionated soy product.) Sprouted soy does not contain the same allotype of provocative allergens common to soybean products. *COMMENSAL BIO-CULTURES* is a special combination of friendly micro-organisms (in a rice starch base) that may be used to establish and maintain healthy intestinal flora. SEDNA SPECIALTY HEALTH PRODUCTS, P.O. Box 1453, Andrews, NC, 28901 (800)-223-0858

SUPER ANTIOXIDANT. *ActiVin™* is a new, all-natural super antioxidant ingredient extracted from red grape seeds. University studies show that the antioxidant activity of ActiVin is significantly greater than that of vitamins E, C and beta-carotene. ActiVin is made by a totally new, natural extraction method which does not use toxic chemicals. The result is a product that's safe and environmentally friendly to produce. INTERHEALTH NUTRITIONALS., 1320 Galaxy Way, Concord, CA 94520 (800)-783-4636

"NUTRI-TECH" THE ULTIMATE WATER FILTRATION SYSTEM. Pure water is an essential element for good health, Carico International, a leader in health products for 30 years, has developed a "POINT OF USE" system with a unique design that has no moving parts nor requires electricity. It incorporates a multi-stage technology including sub-micron ceramic and selective adsorbents to address all priority pollutants including micro-organisms. In addition, the entire system is enclosed in surgical stainless steel with a cleanable, removable cartridge. Comes with installation kit and video. CARICO INTERNATIONAL, 50 Lisbon Pl., Staten Island NY 10306-2456 (888)-4CI-PURE (424-7873) or (718)-667-7022

CHROMIUM AND ZINC SUPPORT MINERALS. *ChromeMate®*, a patented form of chromium shown to be safer and more effective than other types of chromium, is an essential mineral for energy production, appetite control and lower cholesterol. *L-OptiZinc®* is the most potent antioxidant zinc supplement available. It is the only premium zinc supplement FDA-approved safe for human nutrition. INTERHEALTH NUTRITIONALS., 1320 Galaxy Way, Concord, CA 94520 (800)-783-4636

DETOXIFICATION AND INTERNAL CLEANSING. One key factor in working with ADD children would be an internal cleansing program which eliminates the possibility of Candida and parasites. *Paragone I & II* is an internal cleanse program designed to eliminate this problem. It combines a safe and natural combination of herbs to gently detoxify the body. RENEW LIFE INC., 460 E. Lemon St., Unit B, Tarpon Springs, FL 34689 (800)-830-4778

TACHYONIZED ENERGY. Profound breakthroughs for ADD. One Tachyonized lozenge of *Sleepy Z* (with melatonin) has shown (in test cases) to eliminate the need for a 10mm Valium. *Tachyonized Silica Gel* taken in doses of 2 drops in fluid twice a day, has promoted regeneration of nerve endings. *Tachyonized Velcro Headband* has proved to be a valuable aid for ADD when one or two 24mm Tachyon Cells are added. These magnify the brain balancing properties of the headband with their direct flow of energy to the lobes of the brain. ADVANCED TACHYON TECHNOLOGIES, 435 Tesconi Circle, Santa Rosa, CA 95401 (800)-966-9341

SUPER BLUE GREEN® ALGAE. Commonly reported benefits: Increased focus/concentration, improved behavior, calm energy, increased learning ability, better disposition/more cooperative, strengthening of immune system, reduction of stress, anxiety and depression. Supplies nearly all the essential raw dietary nutrients that are lost in growing and processing most foods. Wild grown, raw, whole food. The missing link for vital health. Mitch Drake or Sharon Trump, Independent Distributors, 473 Coco Plum Ct., Satellite Beach, FL. 32937, (800)-981-0001/code 99 or (800)-399-2024/ code 55

DRUG-FREE RELIEF FOR ADD. Only the finest bio-engineered and Psychopharmacologically tested products available for naturally managing ADD & ADHD. Rosavin™, (special Rhodiola rosea extract), adjusts the chemicals in the brain, balancing the neurotransmitters, and is included with Rhododendron caucasicum and Hydroxycinnamic acid in OPTIMIND. This product increases the length of activity of Rhodiola, helps lower blood pressure and fights allergies and viruses. MEGA BETA 1, 3-D GLUCAN speeds up the production cycle of the immune system to repair itself. CEREBRAL DHA is beneficial for ADD and includes DHA,EPA, Stearidonic acid, Vitamin E & C. KIDWELL (The original olive leaf extract for kids) is a natural antibiotic. AMERIDEN INTERNATIONAL, P.O. Box 1870, Fallbrook, CA. 92088 (888) 405-3336

GREEN MAGIC. Green Magic is an organic array of 17 superfoods that are blended together fresh every week to provide the body with vital nutrients that nourish every cell in the body, and stimulate the production of new immune cells. These nutrients are virtually absent from the food that is available today. These ingredients are chosen from the most nutrient rich soils from all over the world, and are designed to work synergistically with each other. NEW SPIRIT NATURALS, 3684 Misty Lane, Aptos, CA 95003 (888)-MAGIC-82 (624-4282) Fax (408)-479-1231 E-mail: magic @rydon.com

BRAIN FUNCTION SUPPORT. Numerous studies confirm a link between nutrition and brain function, which show that deficiencies in certain essential fatty acids may be tied to specific behavioral traits consistent with ADHD and other learning difficulties. *Efalex™ Focus* provides High DHA Tuna Oil, GLA rich Efamol Evening Primrose Oil and powerful antioxidants Thyme Oil & vitamin E. EFAMOL NUTRACEUTICALS, INC. 23 Dry Dock Ave., Boston MA 02210 Toll Free (888)-EFALEX-1 website: www.efamol.com

ECONOMICAL AIR PURIFIERS. The EPA has labeled indoor air pollution the #1 environmental health threat in America. Children, and also people with compromised immune systems, can be more severely affected by indoor air pollution. Purify your air. Toxic gases, chemicals, odors, bacteria, mold, smoke, pollen, pet odors and dust reduced. Portable units make fresh air the way nature does. Environmentally friendly and economical....no filters to continually replace. Whole house and small space units available. DEBBIE MARSH, ALPINE INDEPENDENT DISTRIBUTOR, Air Quality Consultant, 512 Cleveland St., #193, Clearwater, FL 34615 (800)-581-4244

NATURAL ALTERNATIVES TO DRUGS. *BACK TO BALANCE* is a unique blend of amino acids, vitamins and minerals. It is a safe and effective alternative for children and adults who suffer from ADD/ADHD, panic attacks, anxiety disorders, depression and more. FOUNTAIN OF YOUTH TECHNOLOGIES, Inc., 6811 Tylersville Rd., Suite 167, West Chester OH 45069 (800)-939-4296

PERUVIAN HERBS ROYAL MACA™. Organically grown in the Peruvian Andes, contains four alkaloids scientifically shown to modulate the pituitary/hypothalamus axis. Clinical results for both children, aged three and older, and adults show increased mental focus, feelings of serenity and well-being and improved quality of sleep. Also available, ROYAL CAMU™, a dehydrated fruit pulp of the camu-camu bush, native to South America. High in vitamin C. Anecdotally shown to be a fast, effective anti-depressant and reducer of hyperactivity. WHOLE WORLD BOTANICALS, PO BOX 322074, Ft. Washington Station, NY 10032 (888) 757-6026

LIQUID CHLOROPHYLL. Discover the natural goodness of Chlorophyll products. Chlorophyll is suggested for anemia, fatigue, inner-ear infections and has a calming effect on the nervous system. *DeSouza's Liquid Chlorophyll* is a versatile product that can be taken as a dietary supplement or used as a mouthwash and breath freshener. It contains no preservatives or flavorings and comes in capsules or tablets. Homeopaths should be aware that this Chlorophyll contains no mint, nor methyl or propyl parabens. DeSOUZA INTERNATIONAL, INC., P.O. Box 395, Beaumont CA 92223 (800)-373-5171

TASTY OMEGA-3 PRODUCT. *Essential Balance, Jr.*, for children with A.D.H.D., is a tasty blend of essential fatty acids which contains a scientifically formulated blend of flax, sunflower, pumpkin, borage and sesame oils. It's unique formula, with a natural butterscotch flavor contains the 1:1 ratio of Essential Fats shown to be beneficial for brain development in children. Omega Is the only company that has organic coconut oil, DHA from algae or marine source and organic sesame oil both used in ADHD and autism diet therapy. OMEGA NUTRITION, 6515 Aldrich Rd., Bellingham, WA 98226 (800)-661-3529

WHEATGRASS JUICE. *Sweet Wheat*™, 100% Certified Organic Wheatgrass Juice Powder, is considered a superior supplement. It contains almost every element needed for proper nourishment. Many medical doctors recommend *Sweet Wheat*™ as an alternative to medications. It contains NO fillers, 47% protein, 26% minerals, 23% carbohydrates, is rich in amino acids, antioxidants and chlorophyll. One teaspoon provides the nutritional equivalent of 1 ½ pounds of fresh organic vegetables. SWEET WHEAT, P.O. Box 187, Clearwater, FL 33757 (888)-227-9338 website: www.SWEETWHEAT.COM email: info@sweetwheat.com

MULTI-VITAMIN/MINERAL SUPPLEMENT THAT ARE BOUND WITH ELECTROLYTES. Most one-a-day vitamins are either too potent for the body to utilize at one time or contain such minuscule dosage that they are of little help. Nature's Path, Incorporated's *Mega-Daily-Lyte* is balanced for complete absorption to meet daily needs. It is so well formulated that, in most cases, there is very little need for additional supplementation. NATURE'S PATH, INC., P.O. Box 7862, North Port, FL 34287 (800)-326-5772

BRAIN SYNCHRONIZING AUDIO PRODUCTS. Improved focus, longer attention span, greater calm, reduced need for medication, and increased success in school, are benefits that can be achieved simply by listening at home or at school to *Hemi-Sync®* inexpensive audiotapes and CDs. Brain-balancing sound frequencies played as soft background, help the brain learn how to normalize its functioning. 30-day money back guarantee. INTERSTATE INDUSTRIES, INC., P.O. Box 505, Lovingston, VA 22949-0505 (800)-541-2488

CHEWABLE NUTRIENTS FOR VITAL NEUROTRANSMITTERS. *Restores+*™ for adults and children—available in both original capsules and new *Restores Jr.*™, tasty, naturally-sweetened chewables that kids love. These products contain the specific nutrients the brain must have to *replenish* low levels of vital neurotransmitters, a key element in ADD and ADHD. The result of this is optimal brain function, clarity and focus. Made up of a special synergistic natural formulation of amino acids, vitamins and minerals, *Restores* also promotes increased seratonin, dopamine and endorphin levels. QUEST IV HEALTH PRODUCTS, 2352 Greendale Dr., Sarasota FL 34232 Contact: Mark Rubin (800)-749-9196

Bibliography

-*ADHD: A Demand For A Healthy Diet*, Nutrition Science News, Feb., 1997
-Aihara, Herman, *Acid and Alkaline*, George Oshawa Macrobiotic Foundation, 1986
-*Allergies Alleged To Be Cause of Psychoses*, Medical World News, Jan. 30, 1970
-Anderson, Nina , Peiper, Howard, *Over 50 Looking 30! The secrets of staying young*, Safe Goods, 1996.
-Anderson, Nina, Peiper, Howard, *A.D.D., The Natural Approach*, Safe Goods, 1996
-Anderson, Dr. Richard, ND, NMD, *Cleanse & Purify Thyself*, R. Anderson, 1988
-*Attention Deficit Disorder*, Mosby's Medical, Nursing and Allied Health Dictionary, Mosby Year Book, Inc., 1994
-*Attention Deficit Disorder Part I*, Harvard Mental Health Letter, April, 1995 p1(4)
-Baker, Sidney MacDonald, MD, *Food Allergies, Attention Deficits and Autism*, New Developments, Developmental Delay Registry, Fall, 1996
-Boris, Marvin,BD and Mandel, Francine S., PhD, *Foods and additives are common causes of the attention deficit hyperactive disorder in children*, Annals of Allergy, May 1994
-Challem, Jack Joseph and Lewin, Renate, *The Miracle of Little Andy Alexander*, Let's Live, May 1983
-Crook, Wm. G., MD, *'Timmy, You're Driving Me Crazy!'*, Better Nutrition, Dec., 1988
-DuBelle, Lee, *Proper Food Combining W.O.R.K.S.* Lee DuBelle, 1987
-Fallon, Sally W., and Enig, Mary G., *Soy Products for Dairy Products? Not so Fast.*, Health Freedom News, Sept. 1995
-Frazier, Claude A., MD, *Coping with Food Allergy*, Times Books, 1974
-Gaby, Alan R., MD, *Are Drug Side Effects Being Overlooked?*, Townsend Letter for Doctors & Patients, April 1997
-Gates, Donna, *The Magic of Kefir*, B.E.D. Publications, 1996
-Gates, Donna, The Body Ecology Diet, B.E.D. Publications, 1996
-Gazella, Karolyn A., *Attention Deficit Hyperactivity Disorder, Focusing on alternative treatments*, Health Counselor, Vol. 6, No.1
-Graci, Sam, *Energy Food For Radiant Health, Get Energized!*, Alive magazine #165
-Green, R. Glen, MD, CM, *Hyperactivity and the Learning Disabled Child*, The Journal of Orthomolecular Psychiatry, Vol. 9, No.2, 1979
-Harmann, J., *Immunostimulation by Bacillus Subtilis Preparations*, G. Braun, Verlag Zeitschriften, Medizinische Bucher, 1990
-Hartley, Bonnie, *Is Soy a Ploy? A Look at Some Claims & Research.*, Healthy & Natural Journal, Vol.4, Issue 2.
-Hersey, Jane, *Why Can't My Child Behave?* Pear Tree Press
-Hersey, Jane, *Scientific Studies Linkin Diet to ADHD are Often Ignored*, New Developments, Developmental Delay Registry, Vol 1 No.3
-Howell, Dr.Edward, *Enzyme Nutrition*, Avery Publishing, 1985
-Jensen, Dr. Bernard, PhD, *Chlorella, Jewell of the Far East*, Bernard Jensen, 1992
-Jones, Susan Smith, PhD, *Killer Fats vs. Healing Fats*
-Kusshi, Michio & Aveline, *Macrobiotic Child Care & Family Health*, Japan Publications, Inc., 1986
-Mandell, Dr. Earle, *Garlic, The Miracle Nutrient*, Keats Publishing, 1994

-Mandell, Marshall, MD, *Bio-ecologic Cerebral Malfunction*, American Academy of Environmental Medicine 18th Advanced Seminar, Oct, 1984

-Mandell, Dr. Marshall, *Cerebral Reactions in Allergic Patients*, American College of Allergists, 25th Annual congress, New England Foundation for Allergic and Environmental Diseases, April, 1969

-Mandell, Dr. Marshall, Dr. Mandell's 5-DAY Allergy Relief System., Harper & Row, 1988

-Mandell, Dr. Marshall, *Cerebral Reactions in Allergic Patients..case histories*, Journal of the International Academy of Metabology, Vol, III, NO. 1, March 1974

-Martlew, Gillian, ND, Electrolytes The Spark of Life, Nature's Publihsing, 1994

-Meyer, Patricia, *Diagnostic Drawing by a Child with ADD*, Flower Essence Society Newsletter, Summer 1995

-Mundy, Wm. Lowe, *Curing Allergies With Visual Imagery*, Mundy Assoc., 1993

-Newman, Dr. L., *Make your Juicer your Drug Store.* Beneficial Books, 1970

-Page, Linda Rector, *Healthy Healing,* Healthy Healing Publications, 1992

-Page, Linda Rector, *How to Be Your Own Herbal Pharmacist*, Healthy Healing Pub., 1991

-Rapp, Doris, MD, *Annals of Allergy letter to the editor*, American College of Allergists, Vol 56, June 1986

-Rapp. Doris, MD, *Is This Your Child?*, Wm. Morrow & Co., Inc.,1991

-Rapp, Doris, MD., *Is This Your Child's World*, 1995

-Rowe, Katherine S., MBBS and Rowe, Kenneth, BA, MSC, *Synthetic food coloring and behavior; A dose response effect in a double-blind, placebo-controlled, repeated-measures study.* The Journal of Pediatrics, Nov., 1994

-Sahley, Billie Jay, Ph.D., *The Natural Way to Control Hyperactivity*, Pain & Stress Therapy Center Publications, 1994

-Schmidt, Michael A., *Childhood Ear Infections*, North Atlantic Books, 19990

-Seamens, Dan, *Kids Get Sugar Blues*, Compass, News From the Universe, East West Jnl, Aug, 1990

-Seibold, Ronald L., M.S. *Cereal Grass, What's In It For You!.* Wilderness Community Education Foundation, Inc., 1990

-Stockton, Susan, Olarsch, Gerald, N.D., *Why are Kids Killing...?*, Natures Path, 1996

-Swanson, Dr. James, *A Review of the Studies on the use of Stimulant Medication for Children with Attention Deficit Disorder, Exceptional Children*, Vol. 60, No. 2, 1993

-Tobe, John H., *Milk Friend or Fiend?*, The Provoker Press, 1963

-Truss, C. Orian, MD, *the Missing Diagnosis*, The Missing Diagnosis, 1982

-*Understanding Vitamins and Minerals, The Prevention Total Health System®.* The editors of Prevention Magazine, Rodale Press, 1984

-Upledger, John E., D.O., O.M.M., *A Brain is Born*, North Atlantic, Upledger Institute

-*What is the Feingold Program?*,Pure Facts, March 1997

-Wood, Thomas, M.D., *Upper Cervical Adjustments May Improve Mental Function,* Journal of Manual Medicine, 1992 6:215-216

-Zeff, Jared L., N.D., *The Process of Healing*, Zeff, 1996

-Zucker, Martin, *Learning and Behavior Problems at School and Home*, Let's Live, Sept. 1992

INDEX

OTHER BOOKS FROM SAFE GOODS

· *A.D.D. The Natural Approach*	$ 4.95
· *The Brain Train*	$ 4.95
· *El Método Natural (A.D.D., The Natural Approach Spanish)*	$ 6.95
· *The Secrets of Staying Young*	$ 9.95
· *All Natural Anti-Aging Skin Care*	$ 4.95
· *The Humorous Herbalist*	$14.95
· *Plant Power*	$19.95
· *Self Care Anywhere*	$19.95
· *Effective Natural Stress & Weight Management*	$ 8.95
· *Natural Solutions for Sexual Enhancement*	$ 9.95
· *The High Performance Diet*	$ 7.95
· *Feeling Younger with Homeopathic HGH*	$ 7.95
· *A Guide To A Naturally Healthy Bird*	$ 8.95
· *Super Nutrition for Dogs n' Cats*	$ 9.95
· *The Backseat Flyer*	$ 9.95
· *Nutritional Leverage for Great Golf*	$ 9.95
· *The New Thin You*	$ 9.95
· *Chronic Fatigue Syndrome for the Modern Woman*	$ 9.95
· *Pycnogenol®, The Bark with the Bite*	$ 8.95
· *Audio tapes:*	
ADD., The Natural Approach	$ 9.95
Crystalloid Electrolytes, your body's energy source	$ 9.95
· *Video:*	
Your Child and ADD	$29.95

ORDER LINE (888)-NATURE-1, credit cards accepted
Shipping: $4.00 each book./ Safe Goods, PO Box 36, E. Canaan, CT 06024
website: Safegoodspub.com

BASIC STUDY MANUAL (on improving your concentration and ability to learn)
LEARNING HOW TO LEARN, Bridge Publications
Based on the works of L.Ron Hubbard To order call (800) 424-5397

THE NATURAL WAY TO CONTROL HYPERACTIVITY $ 7.95
with Amino Acids and Nutrient Therapy. By Billie J. Sahley, Ph.D.
To order please call: (800) 669-CALM